MERMAID COLORING BOOK

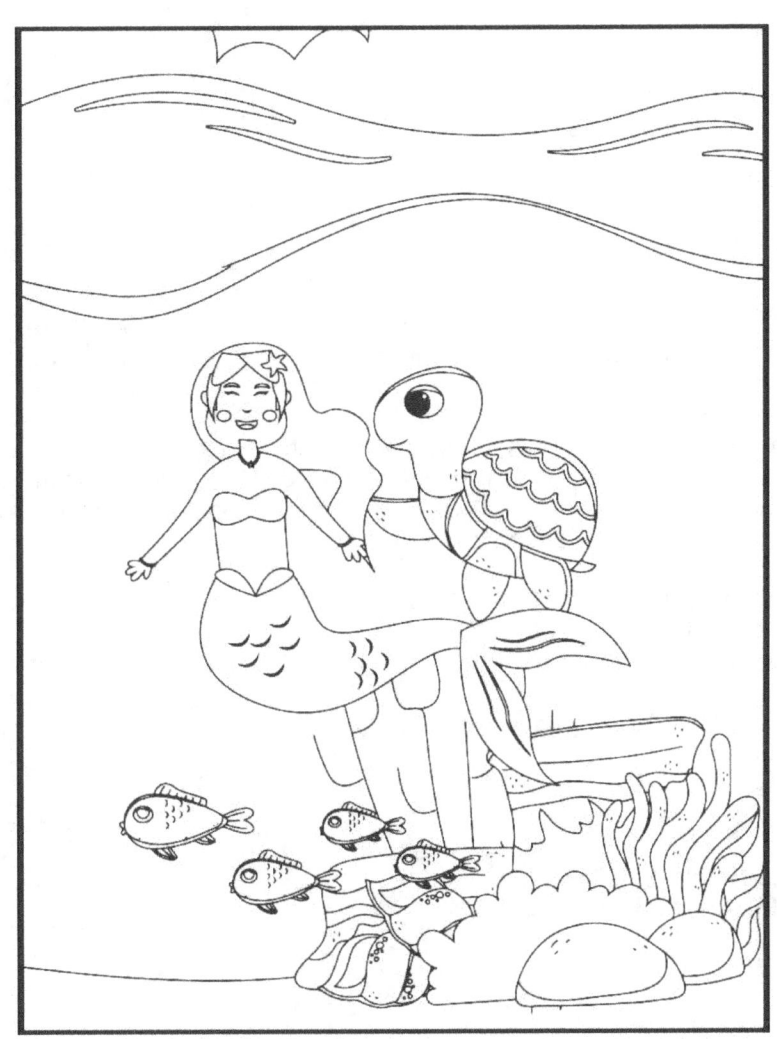

Dr. Melissa Caudle

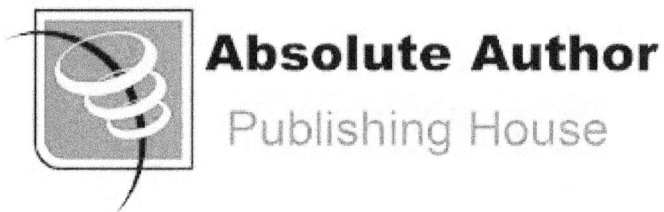

Mermaid Coloring Book

Copyright ©2022 by Dr. Melissa Caudle

ALL RIGHTS RESERVED

No drawing can be copied, printed, or reproduced in any form without the written consent of Dr. Melissa Caudle.

Coloring Hints: It is strongly advised that each colorist place a piece of cardstock or file folder behind each page as you color to avoid bleed through. This is especially important when using markers or watercolor. For two-side coloring books, I recommend only using colored pencils or crayons.

Publisher: Absolute Author Publishing House
Editor: Dr. Carol Michaels
Cover Designer: Dr. Melissa Caudle

Library of Congress Catalogue In-Data Publication

p. cm.

Hardback ISBN: 978-1-64953-671-6
Paperback ISBN: 978-1-64953-672-3

About the Author

Dr. Melissa Caudle is an award-winning screenwriter, illustrator, and bestselling author with over 100 books for adults and children.

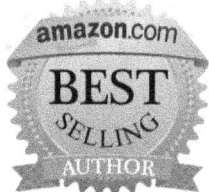

PRINTED IN THE UNITED STATES OF AMERICA

THIS BOOK BELONGS TO:

_____

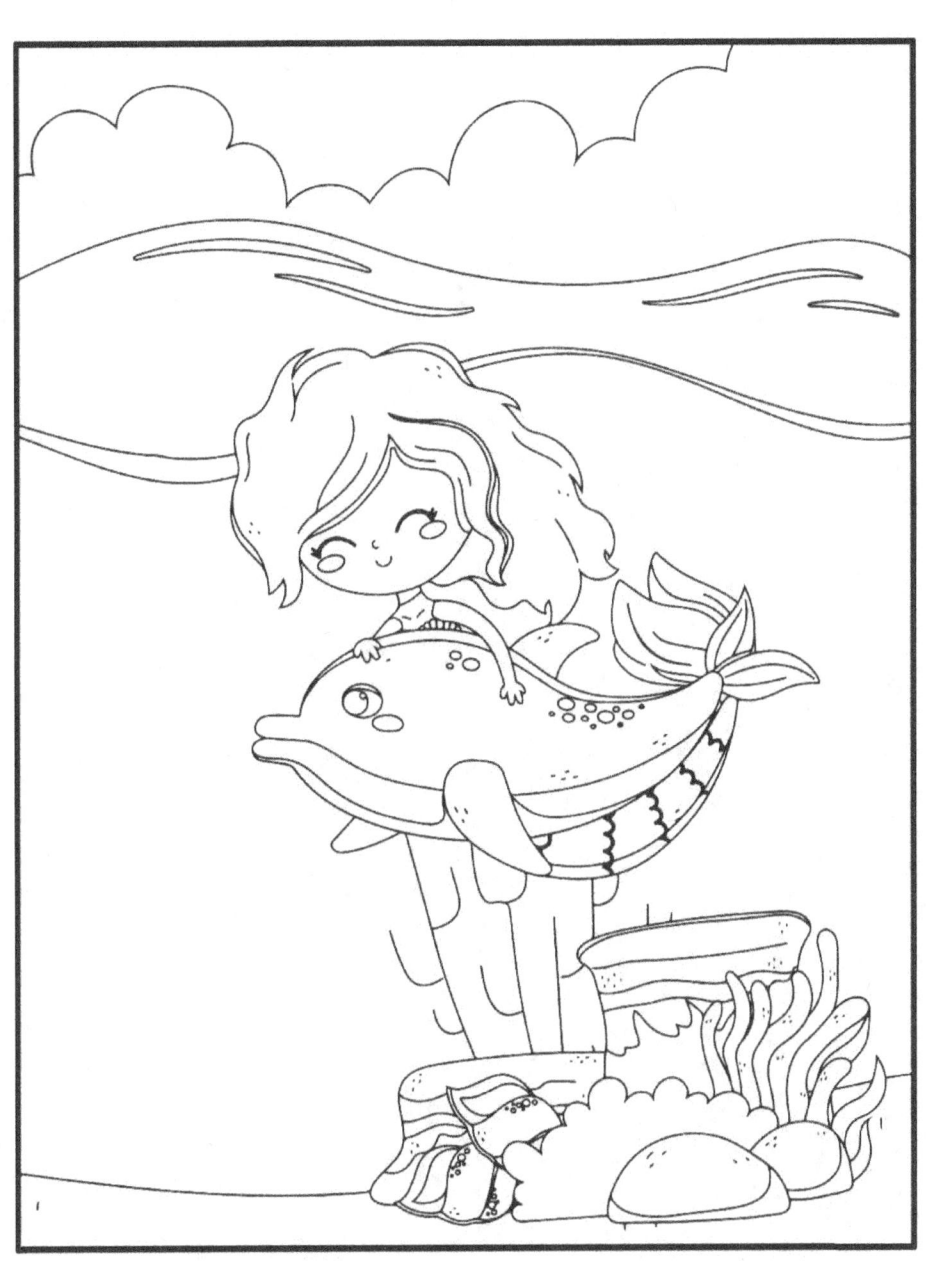

COLOR TEST PAGES

COLOR TEST PAGES

COLOR TEST PAGES

COLOR TEST PAGES

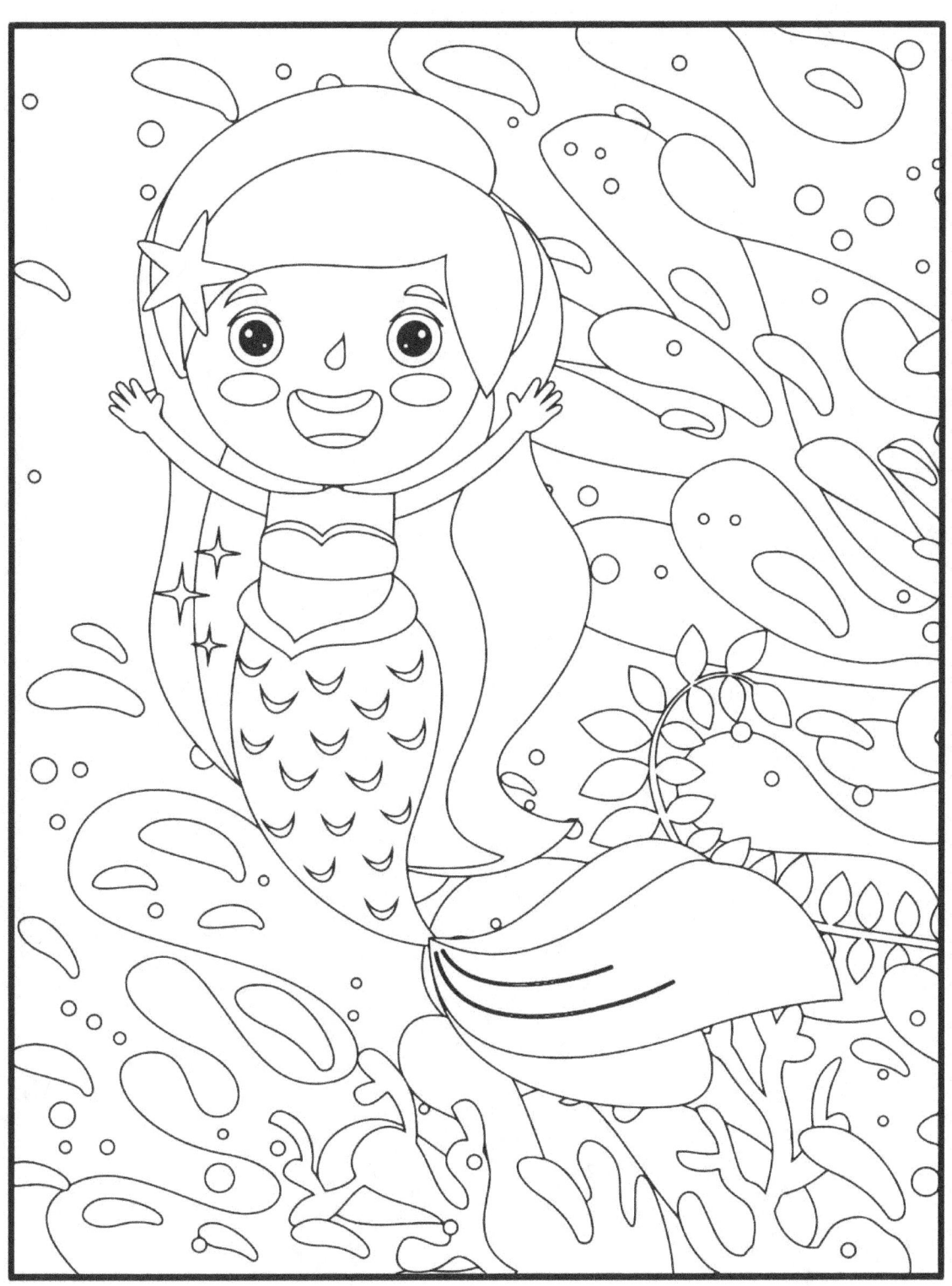

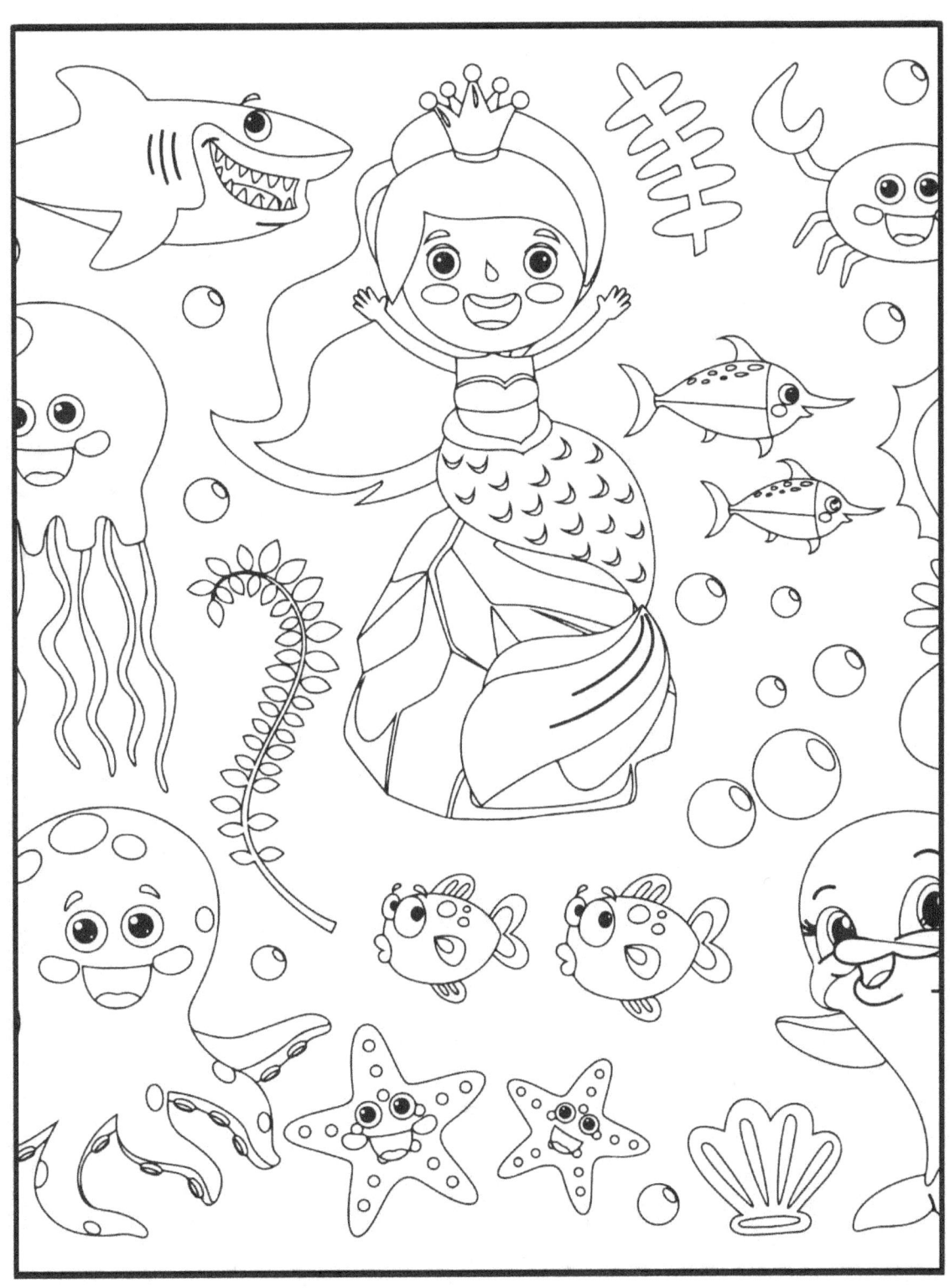

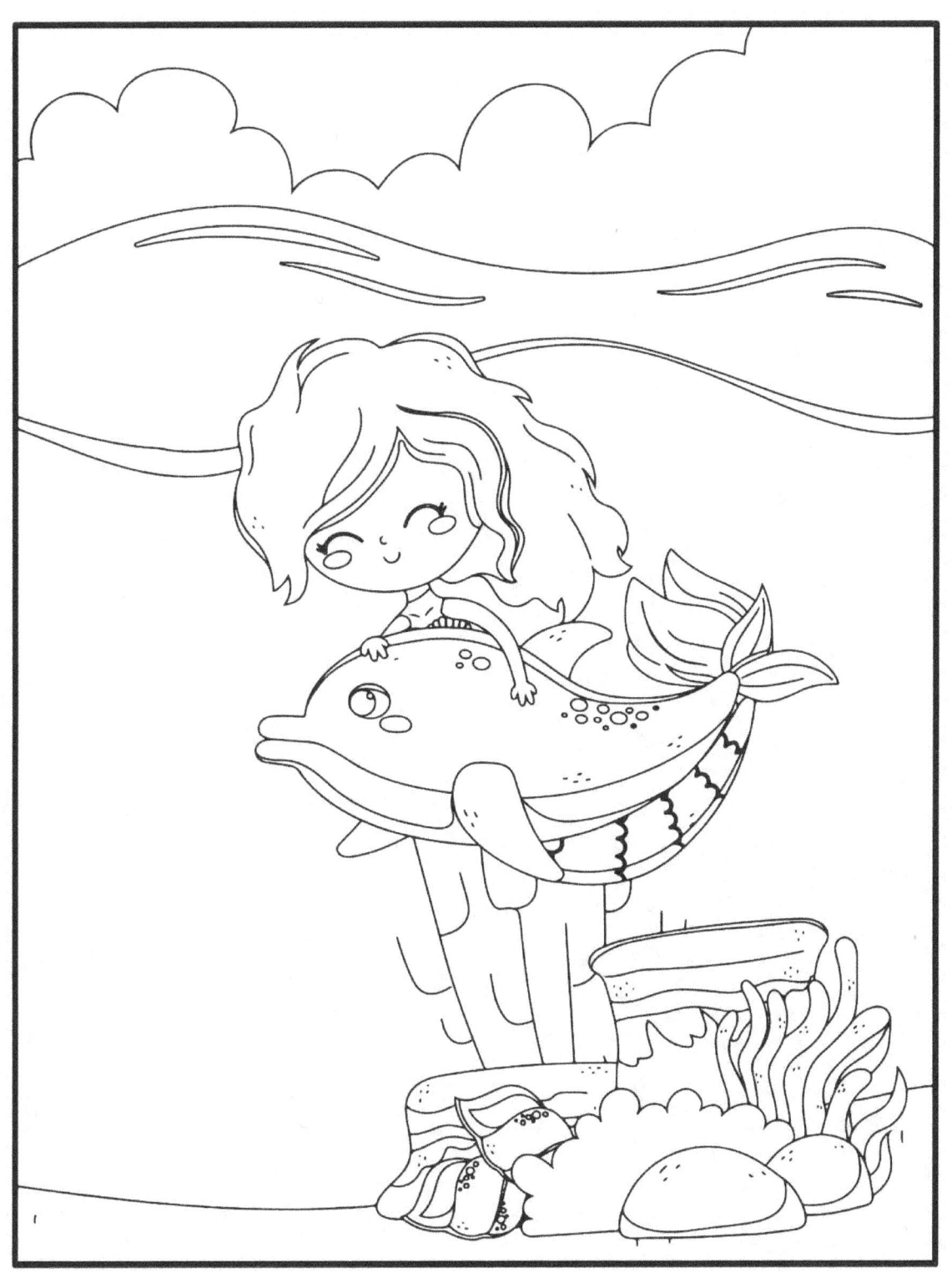

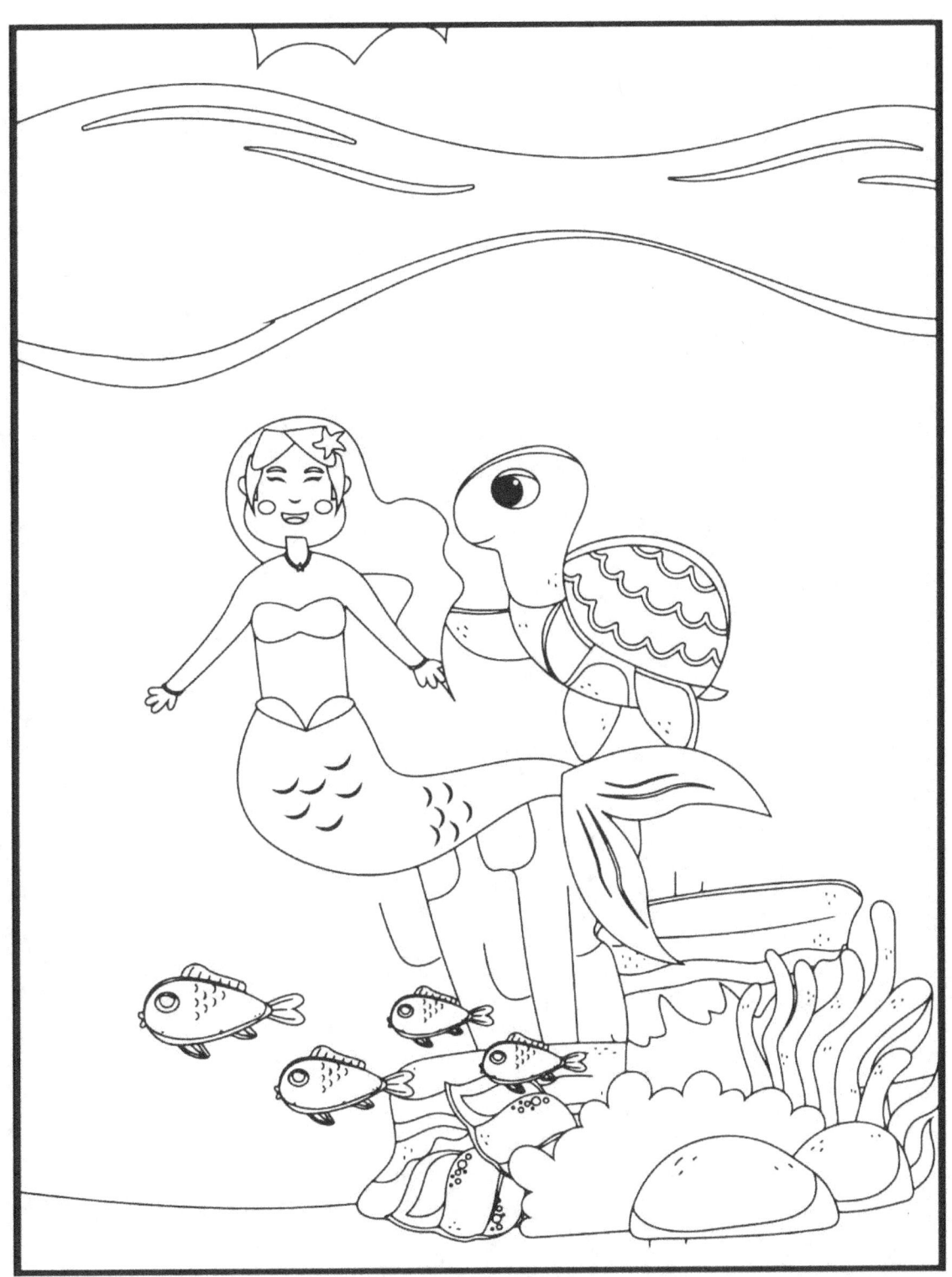

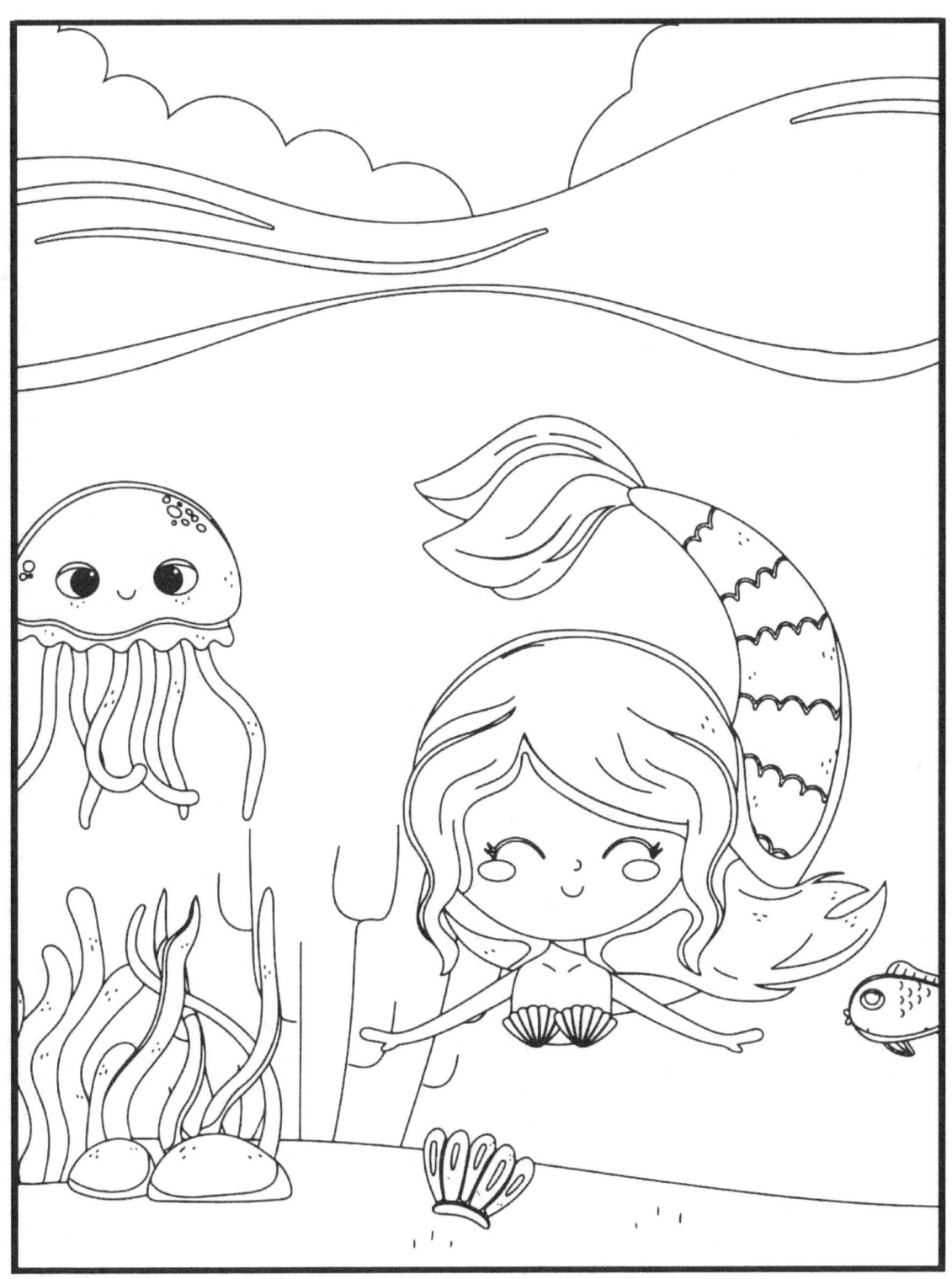

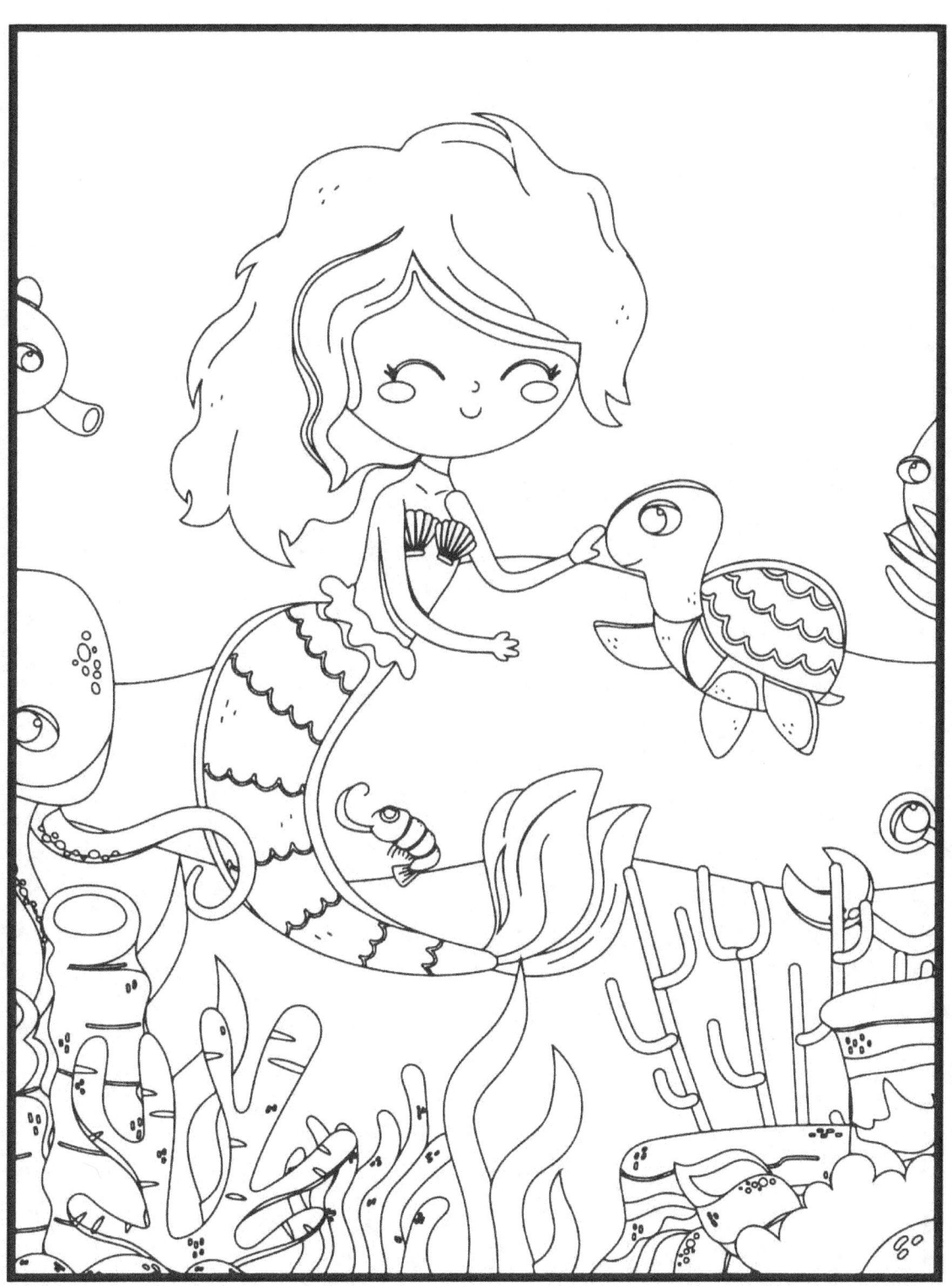

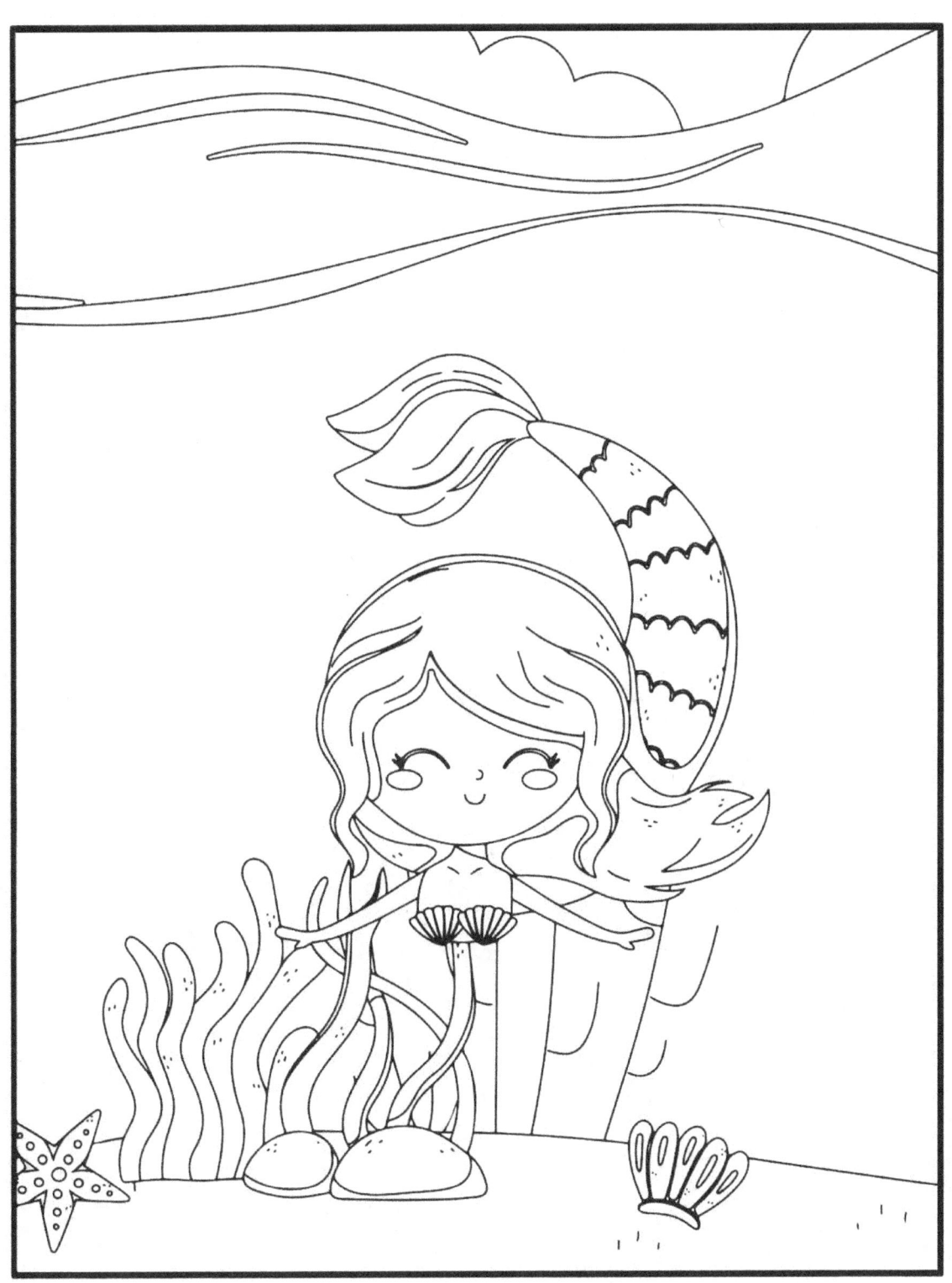

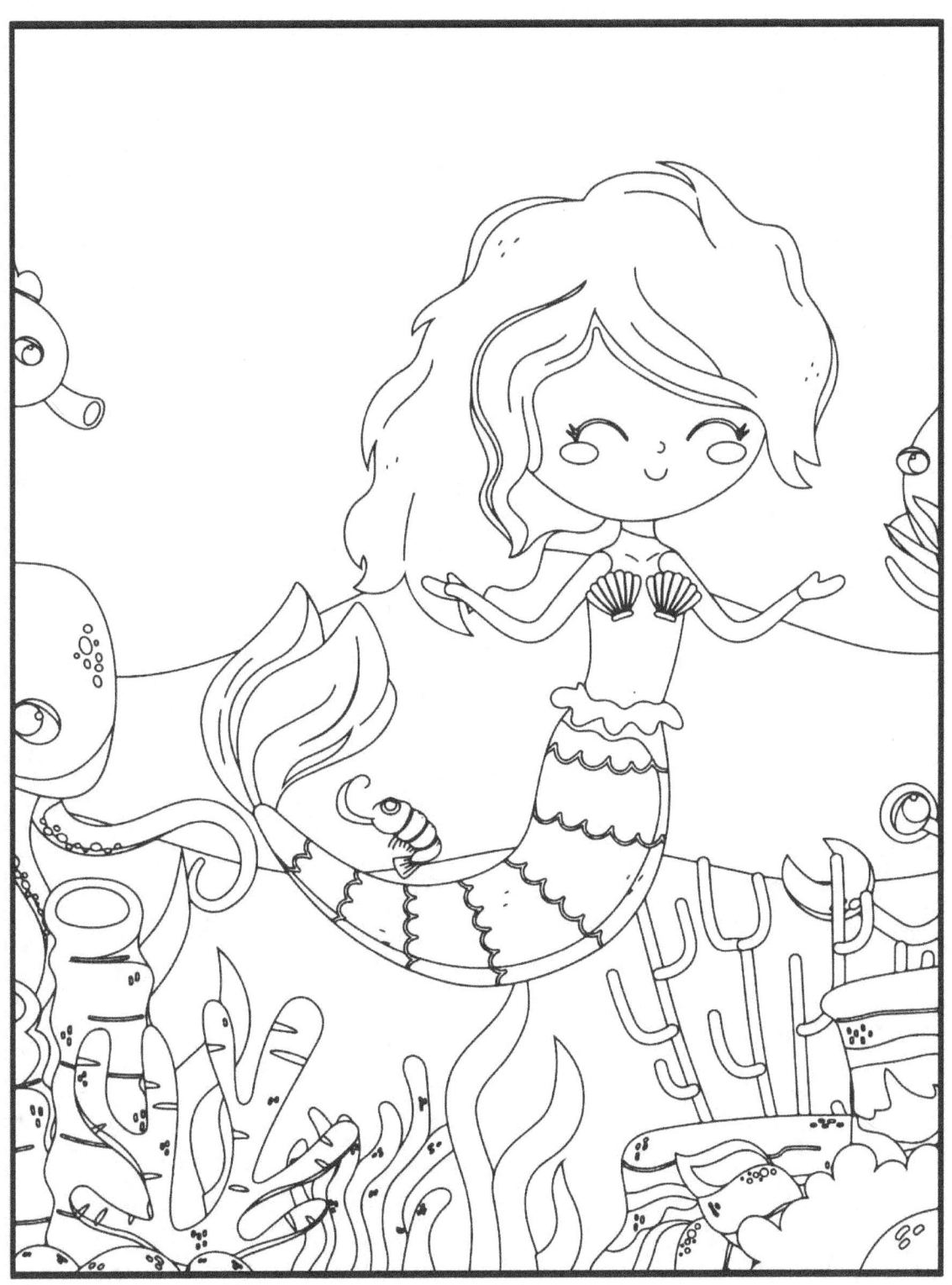

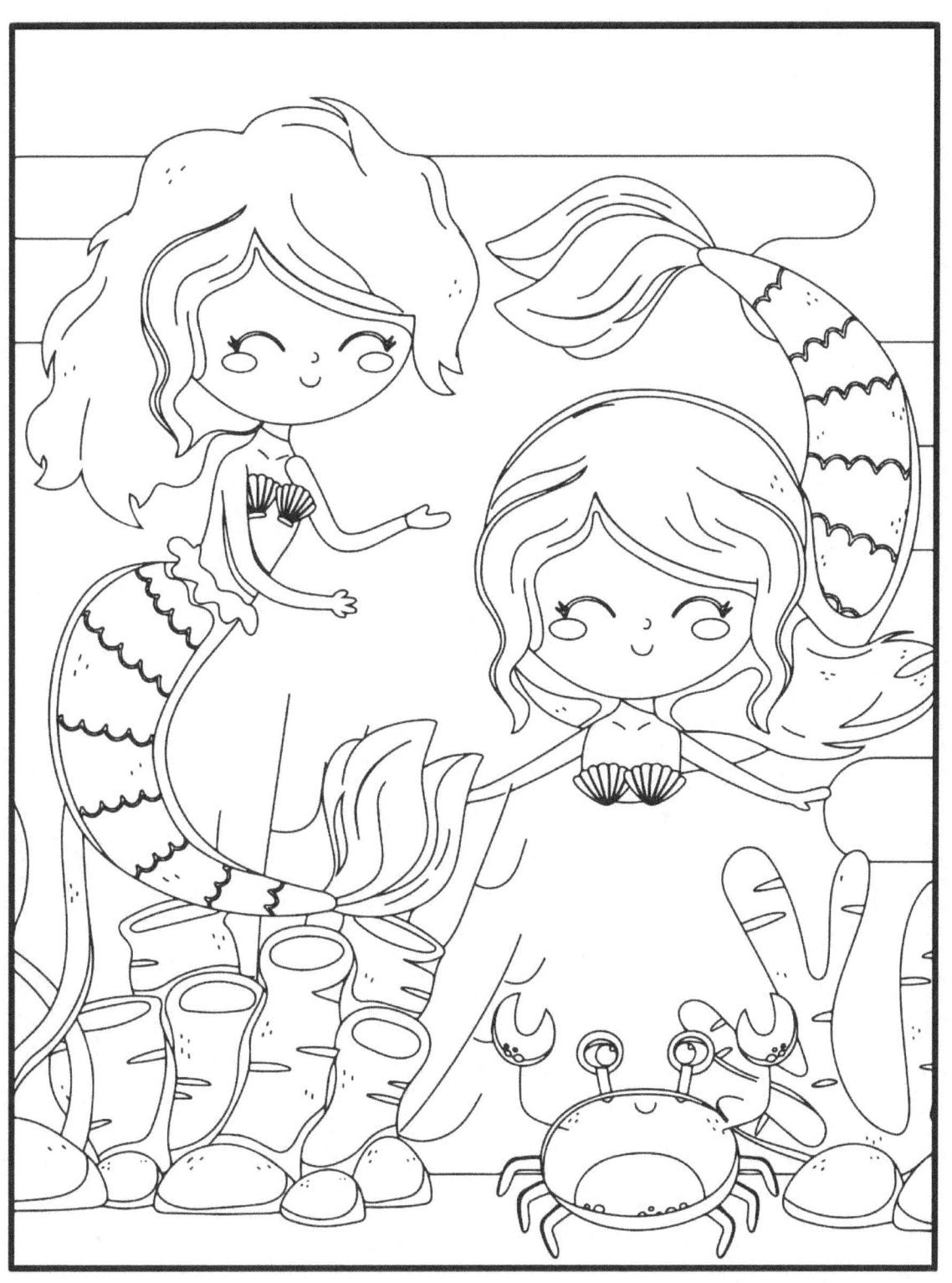

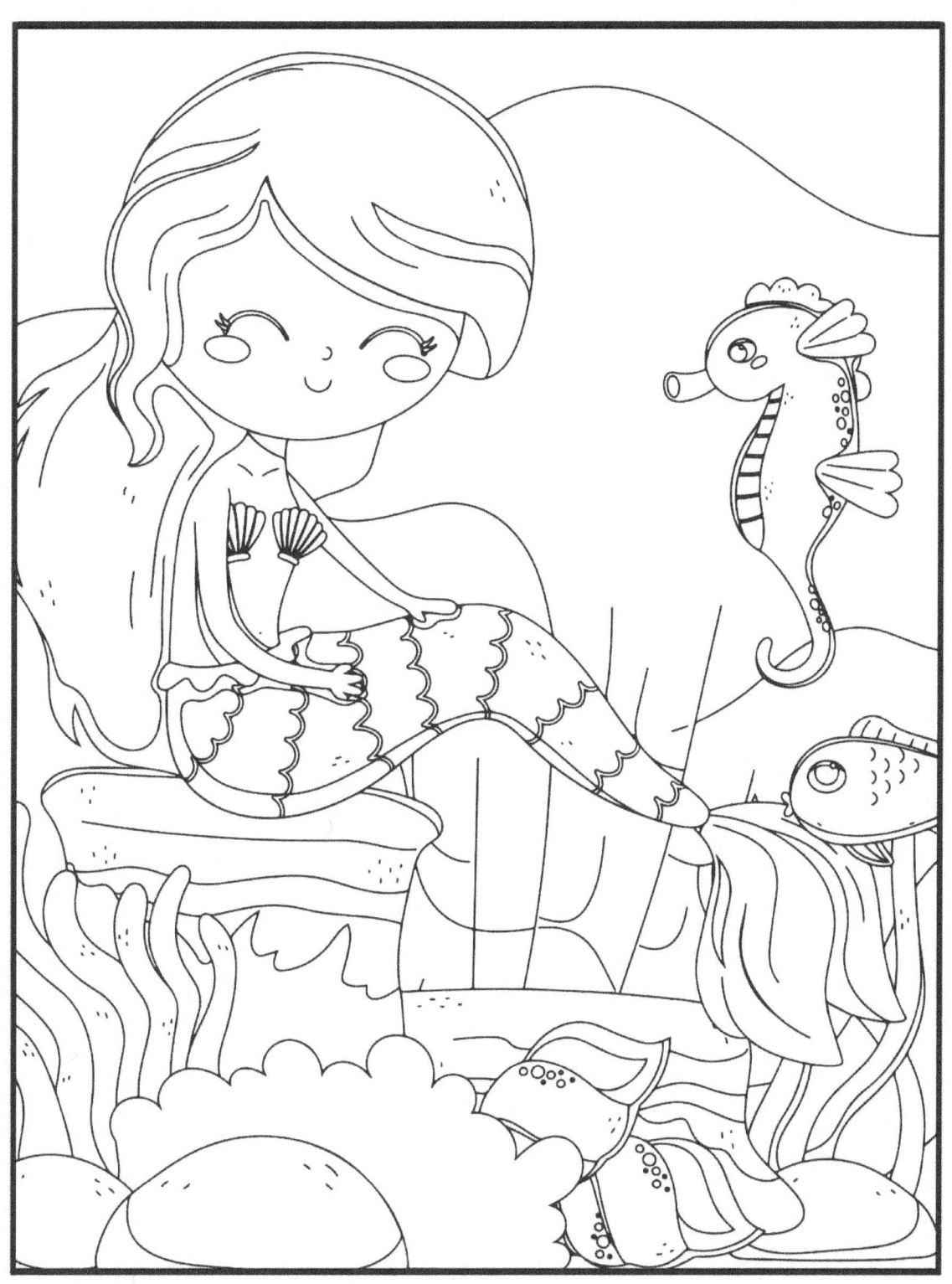

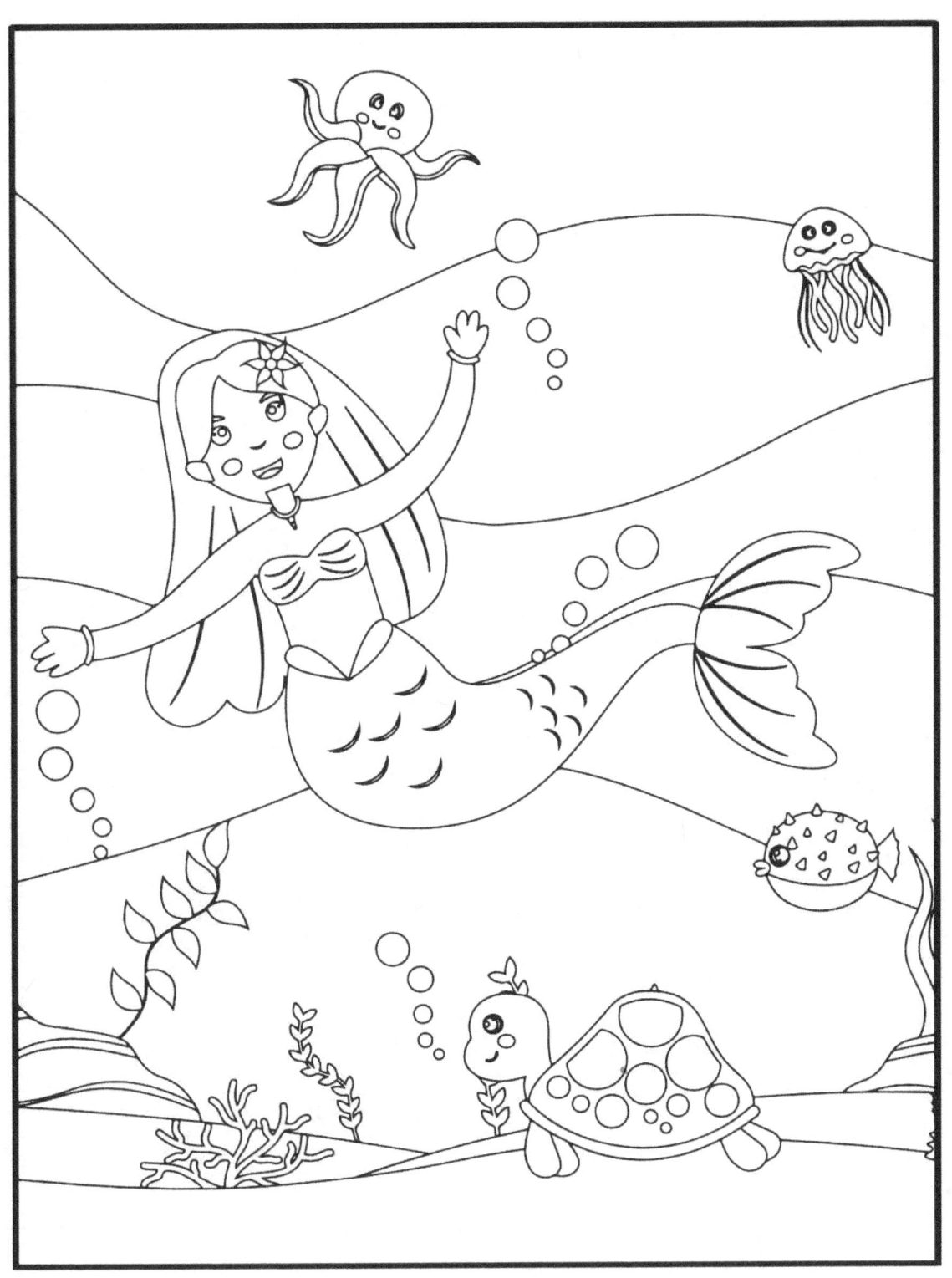

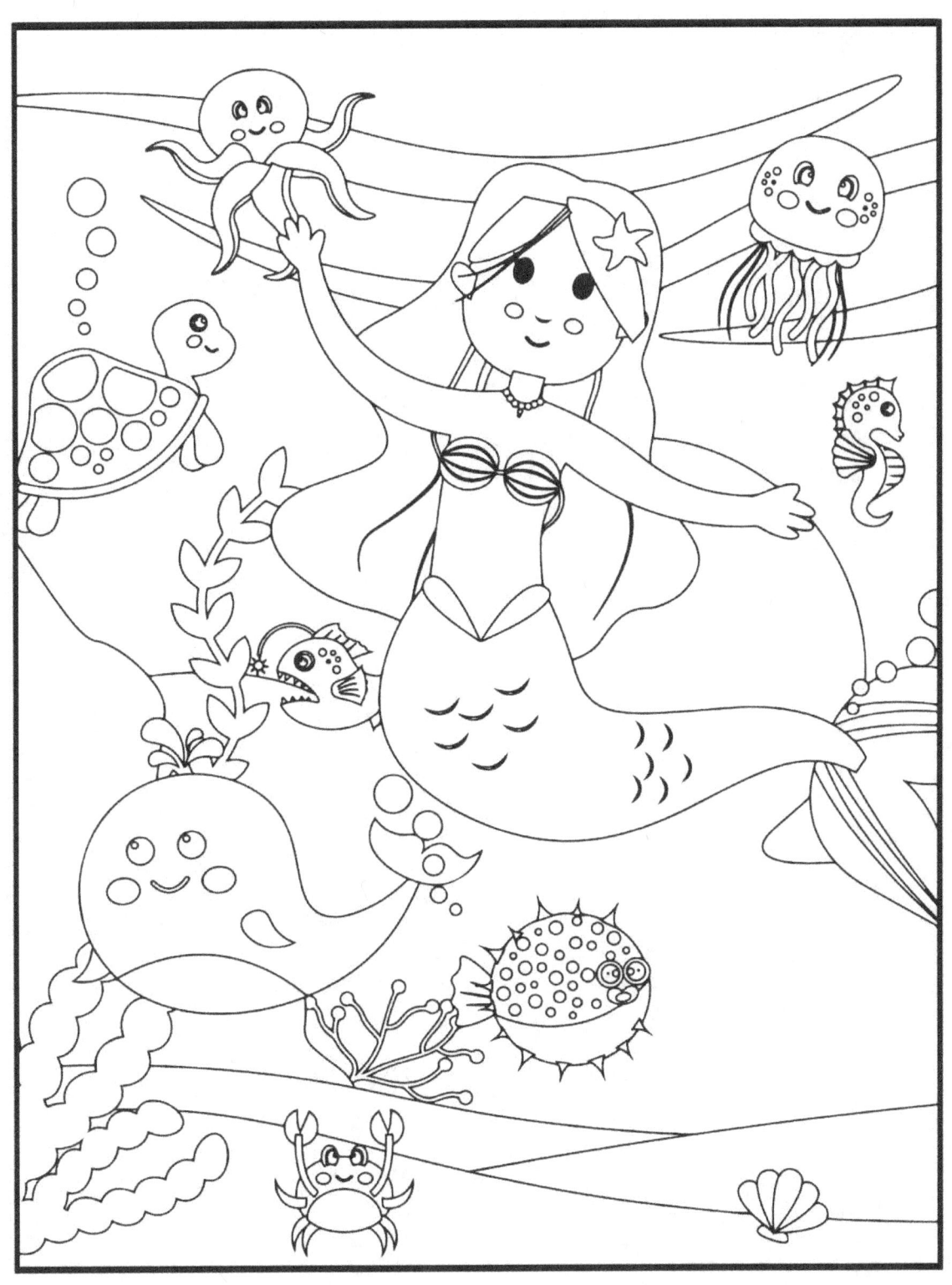

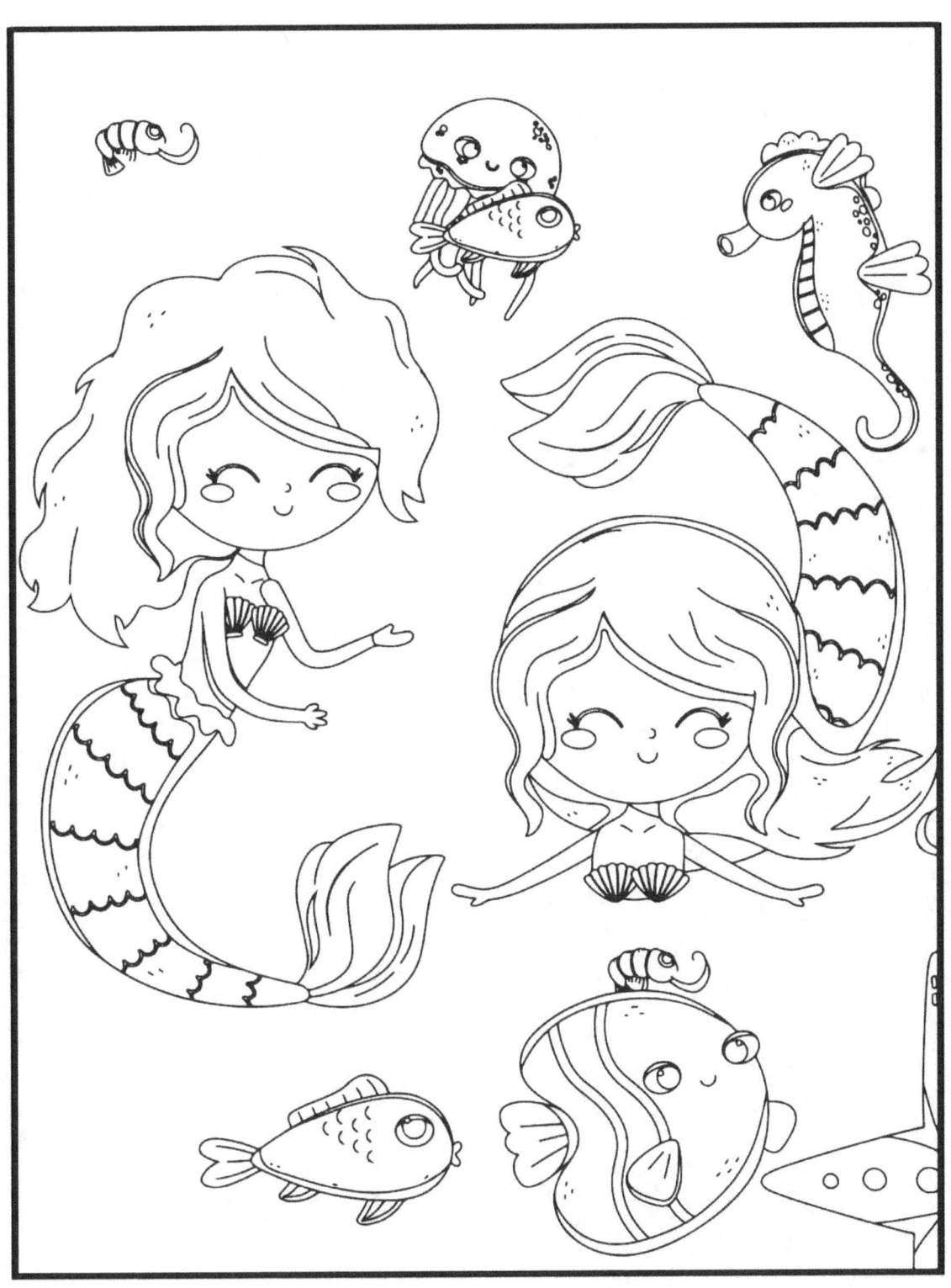

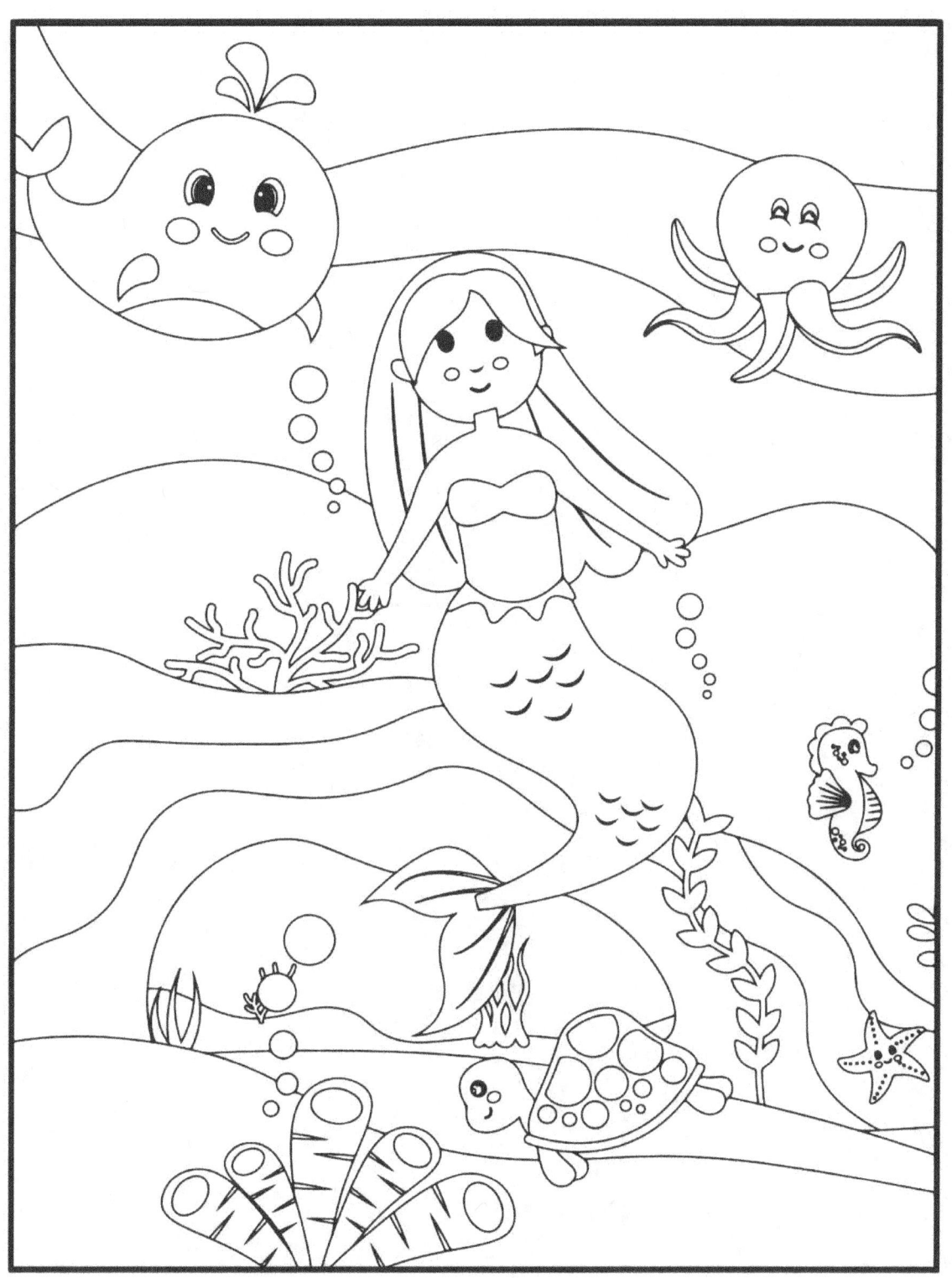

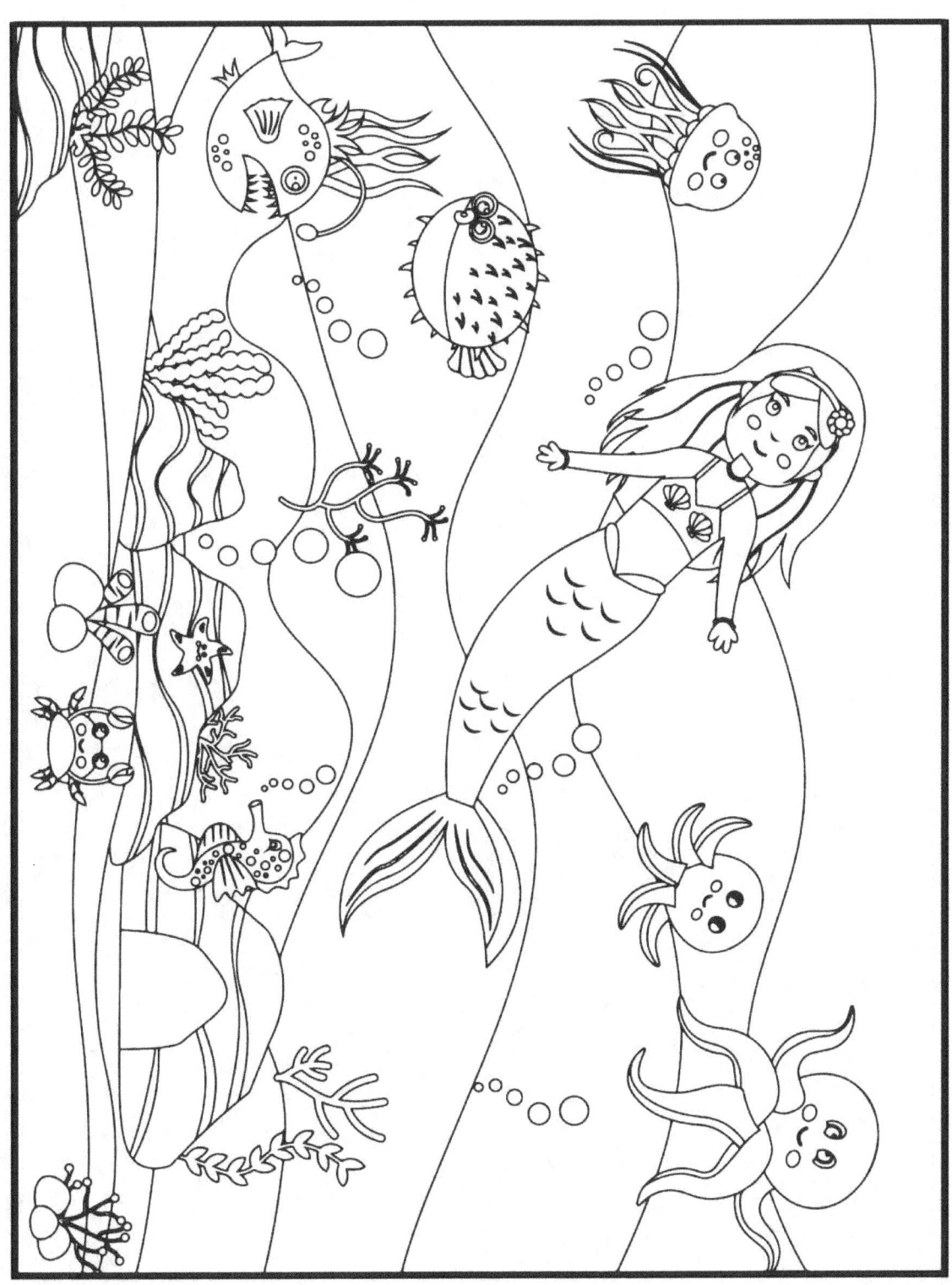

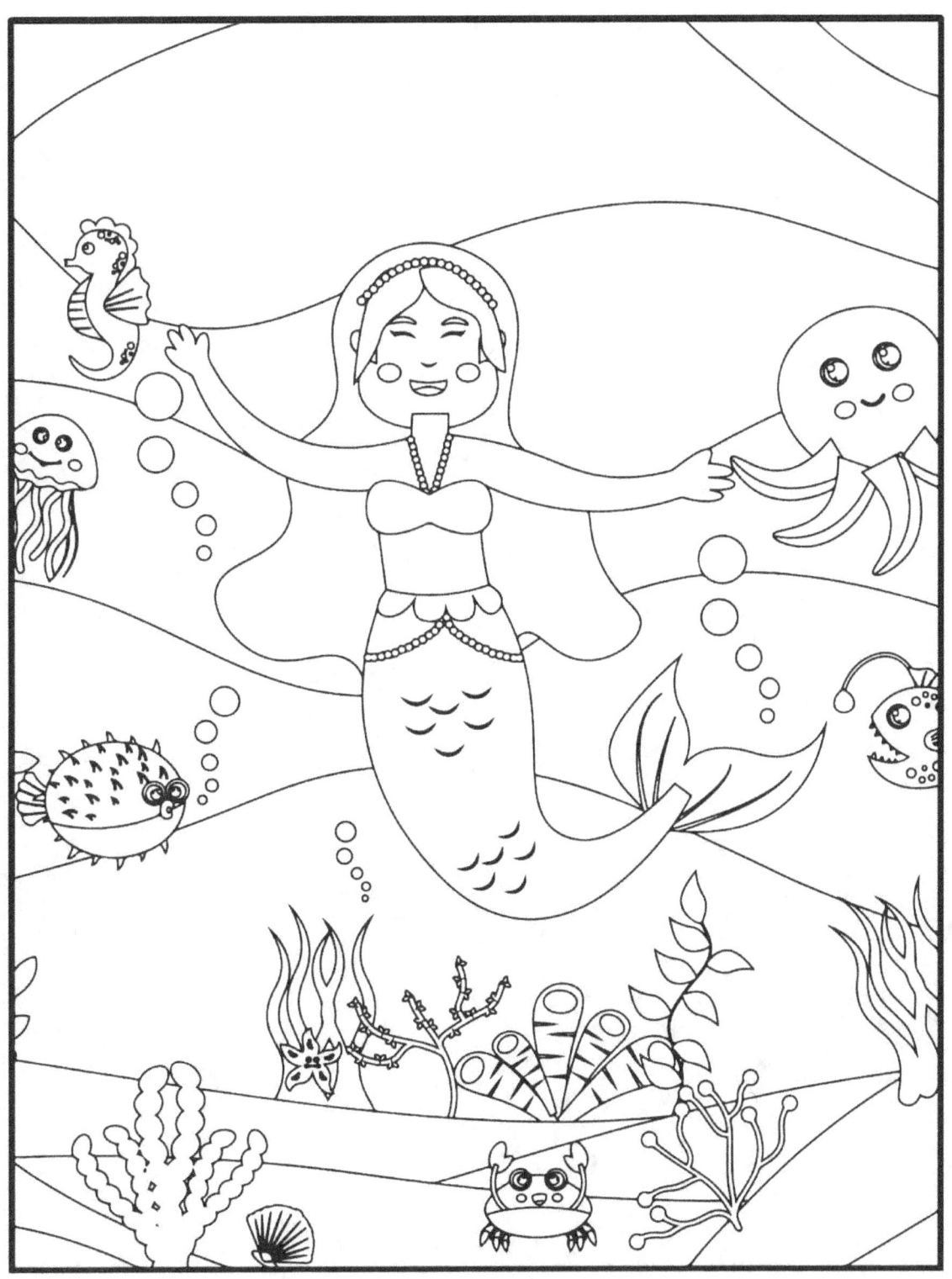

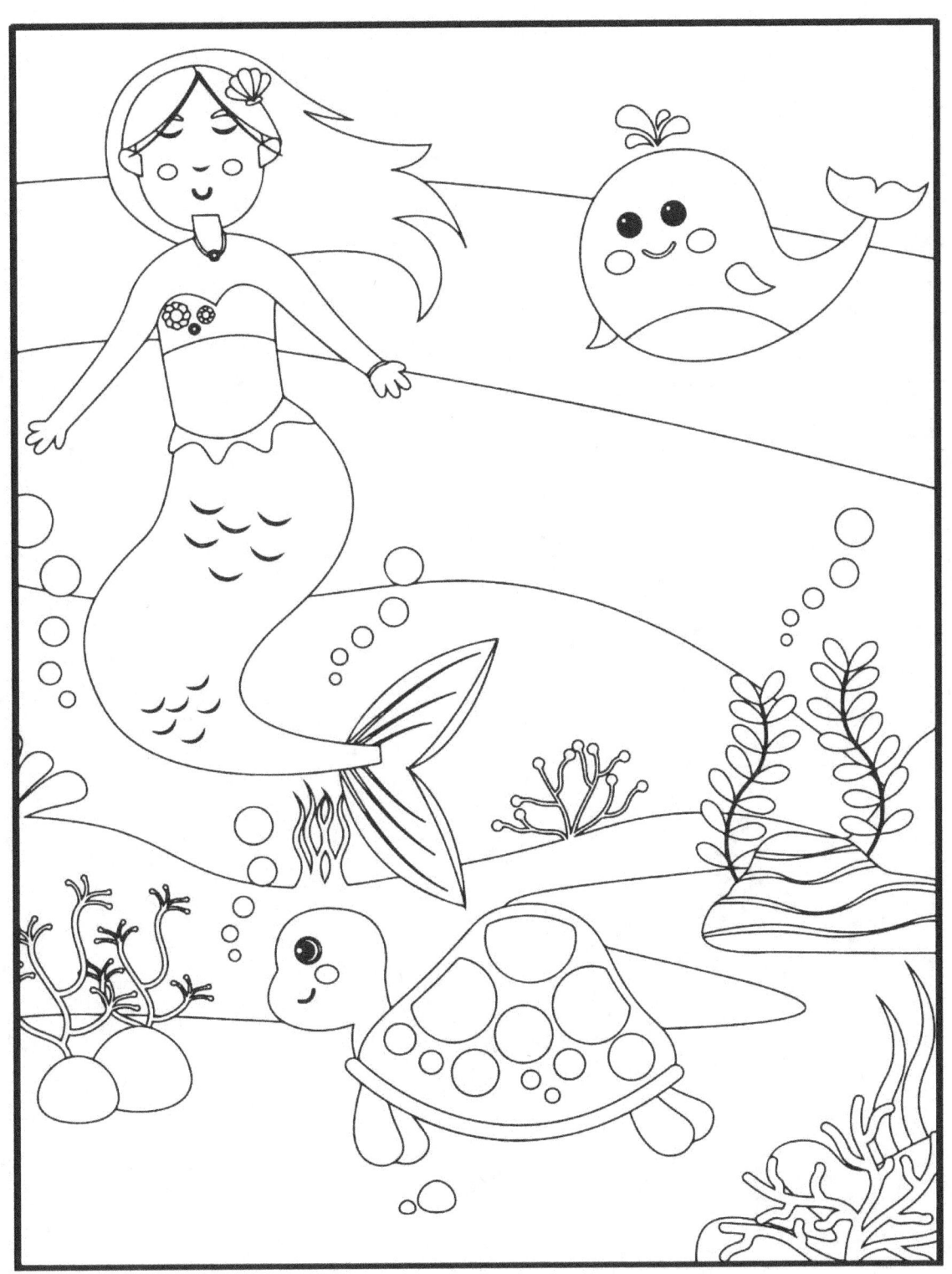

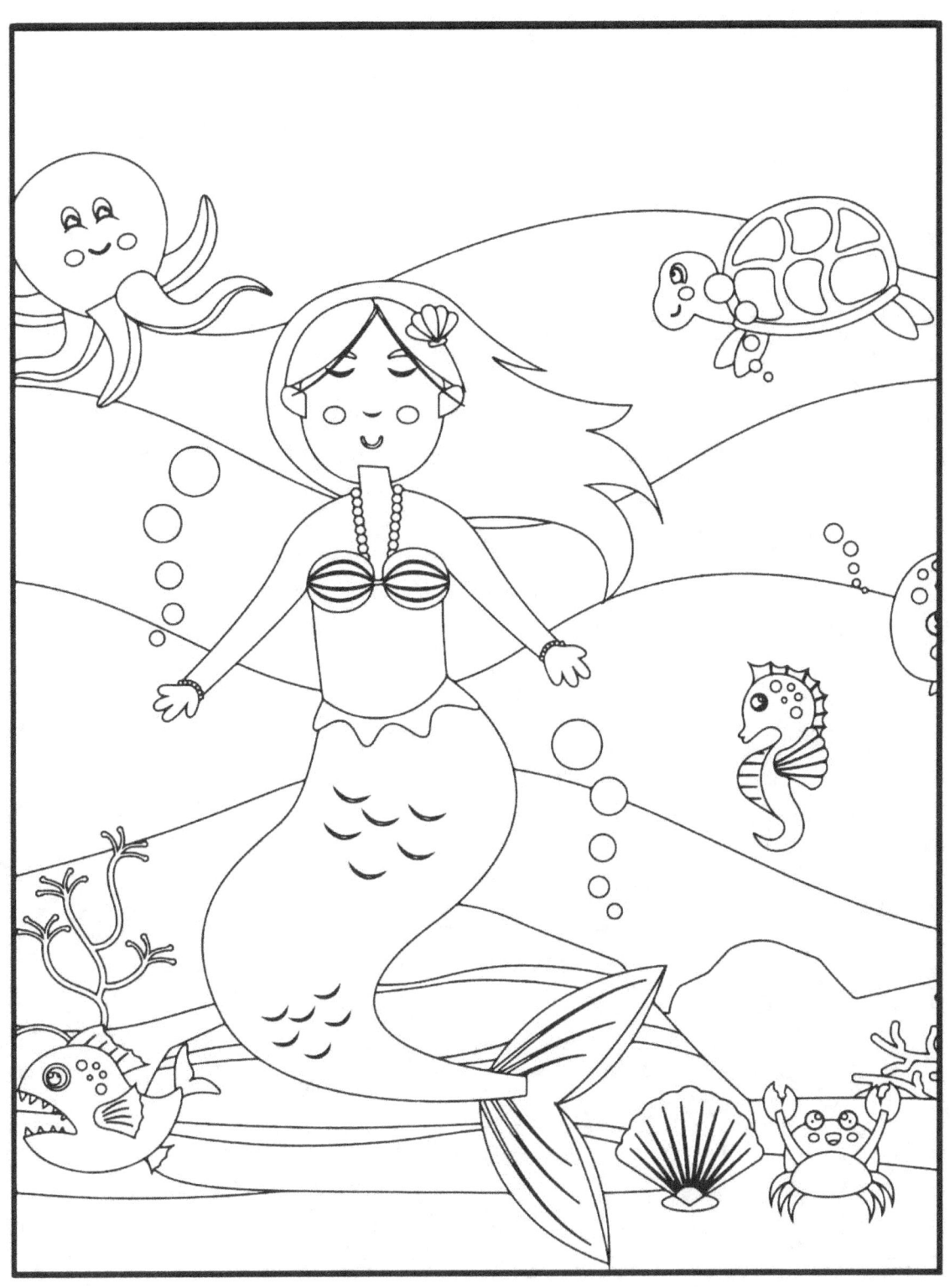

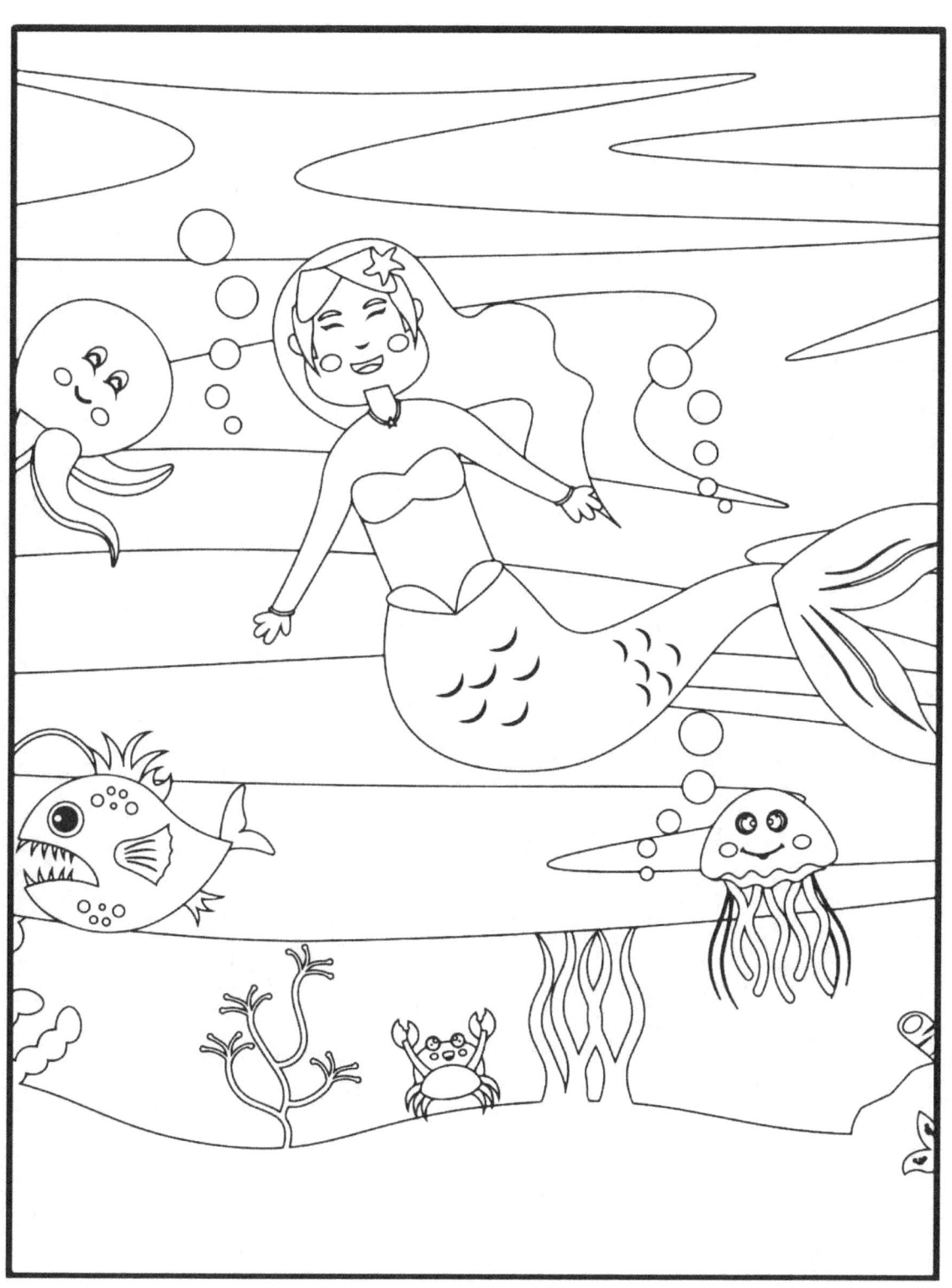

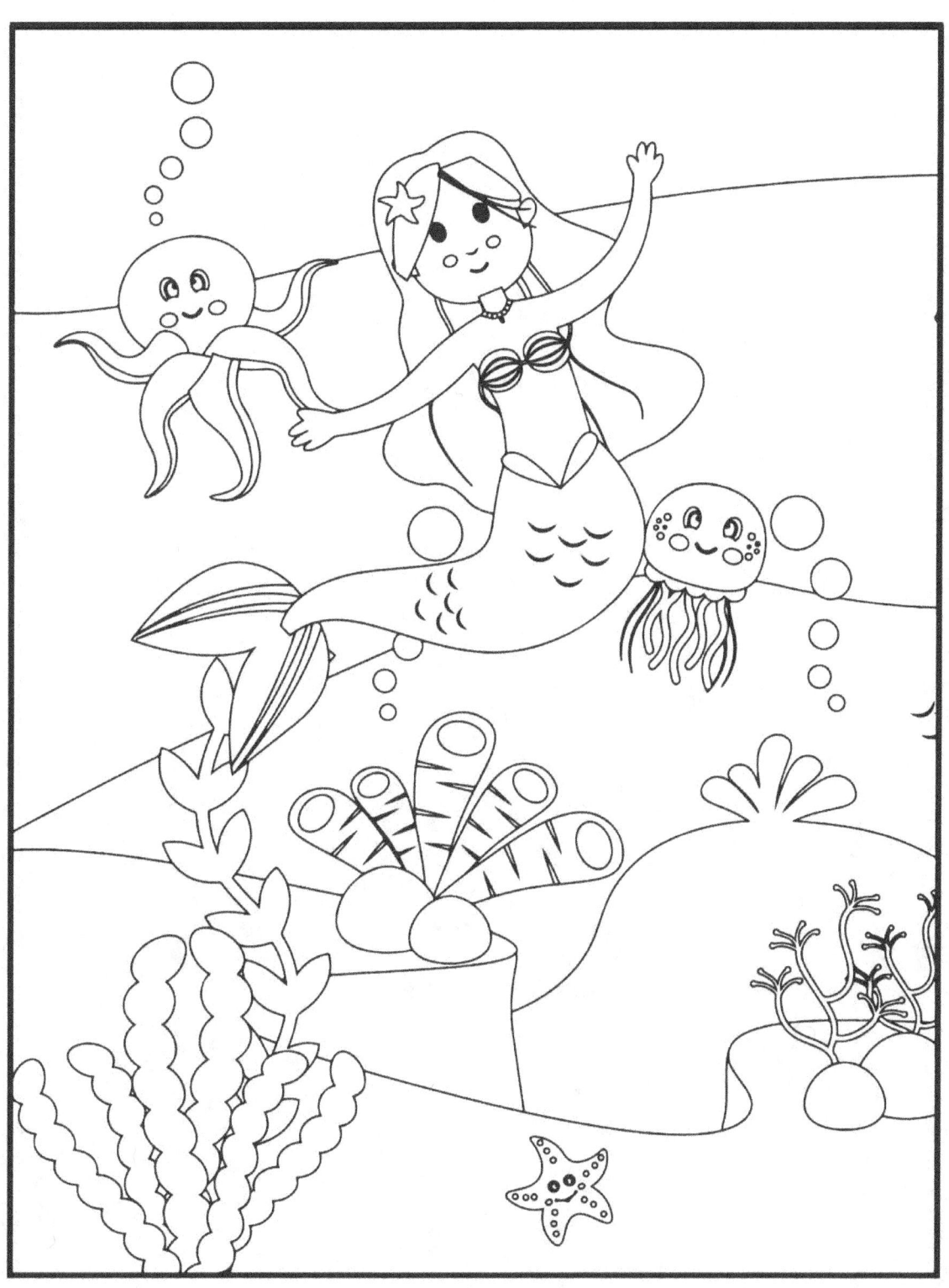

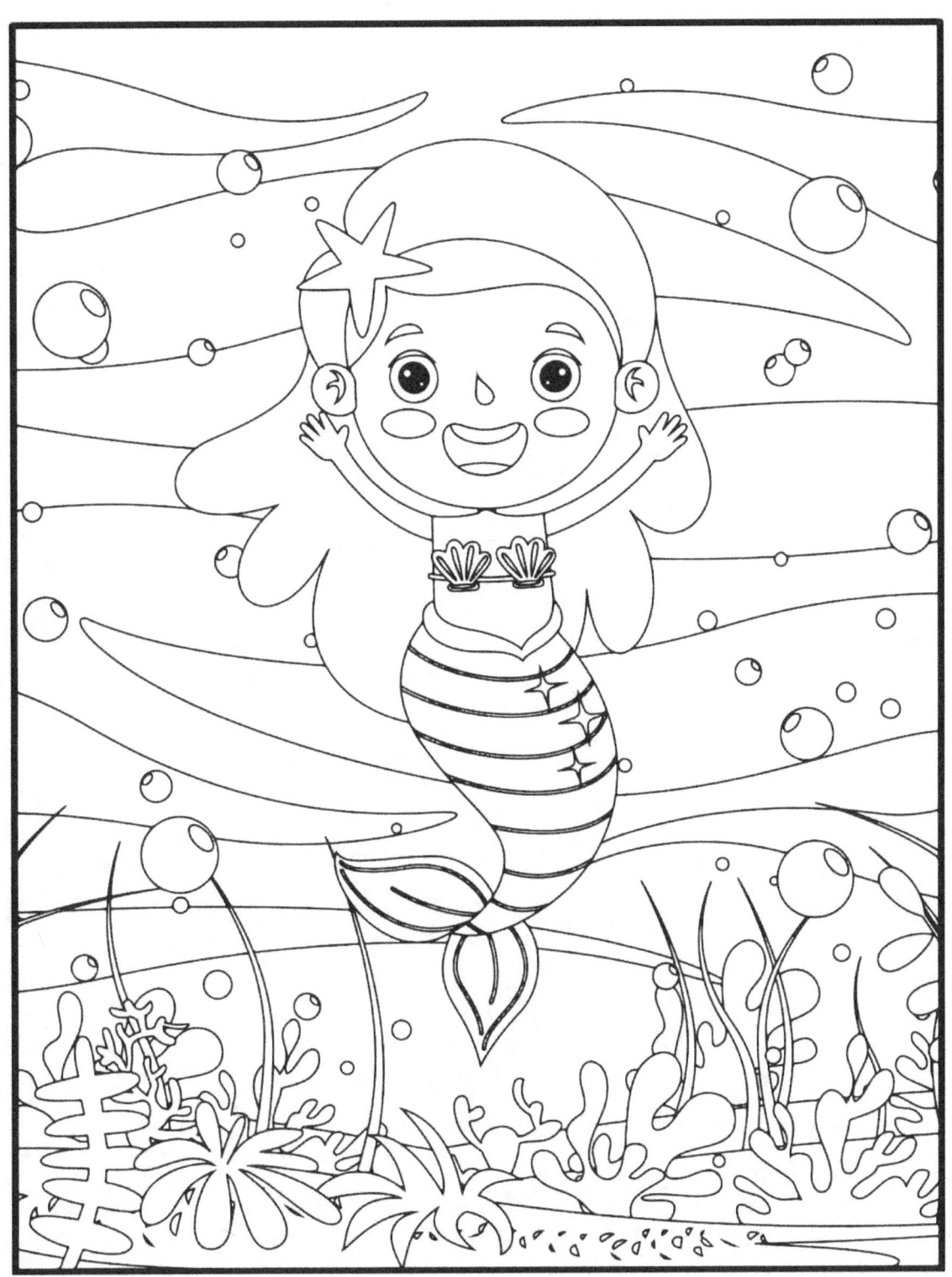

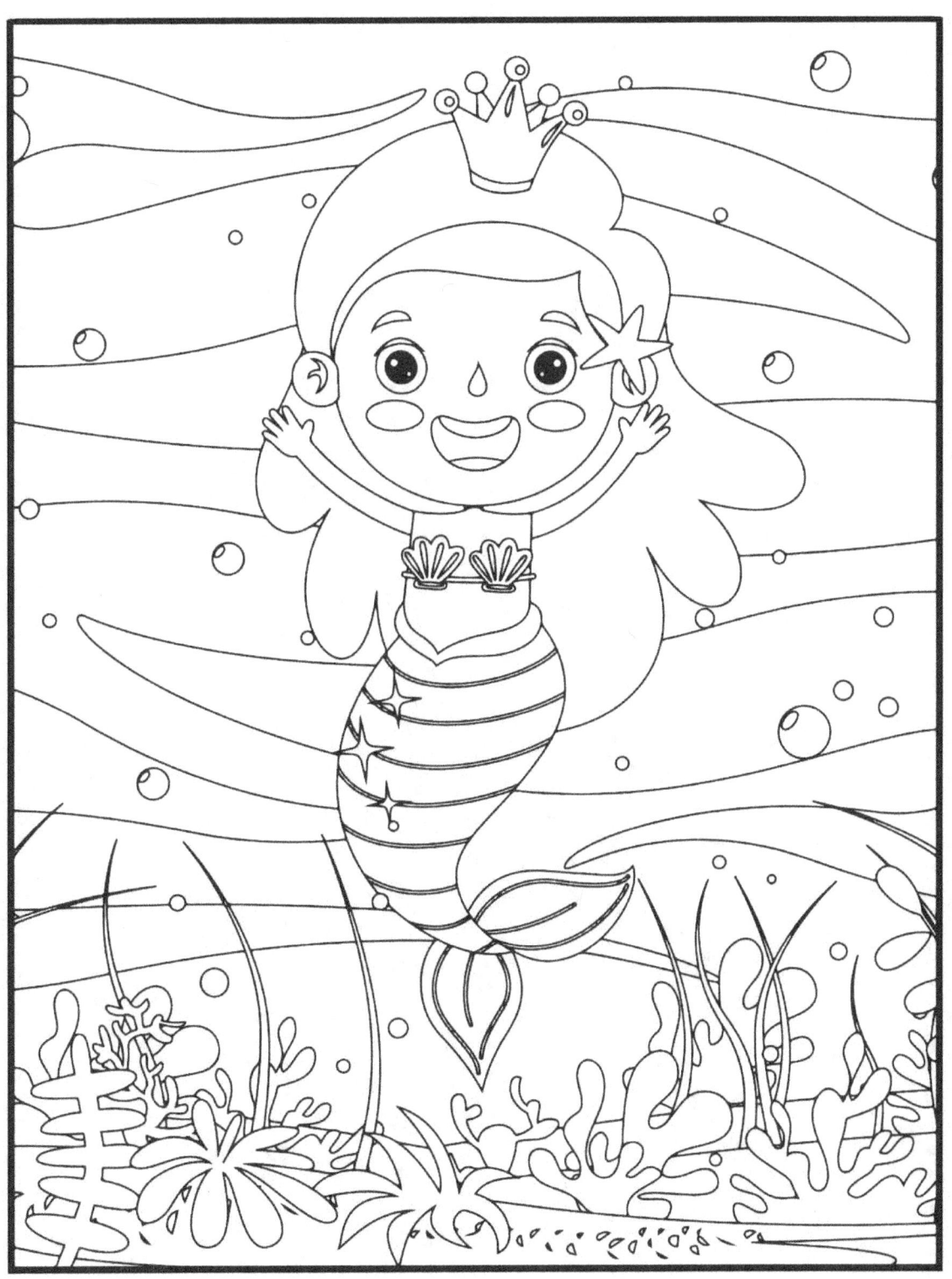

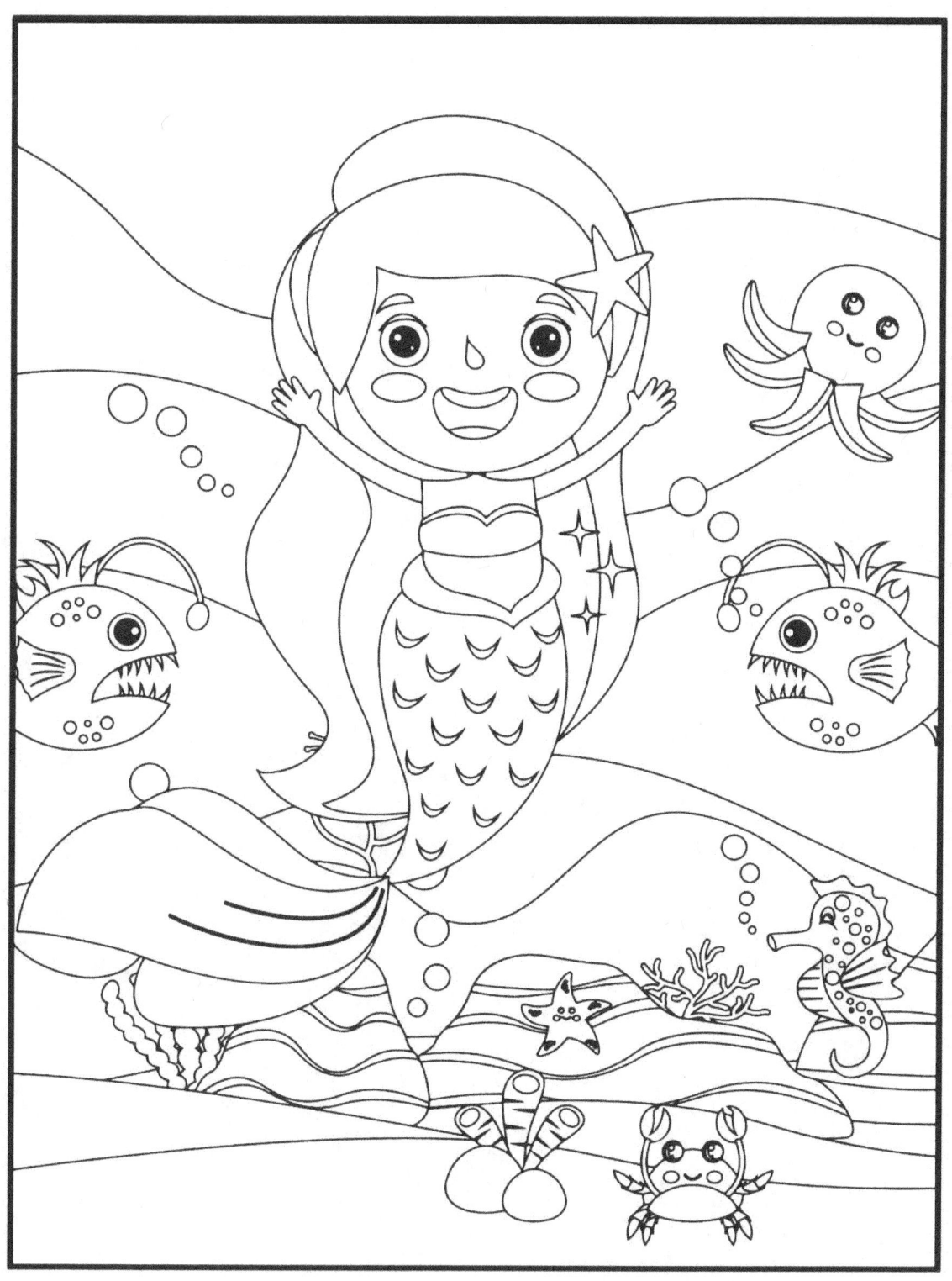

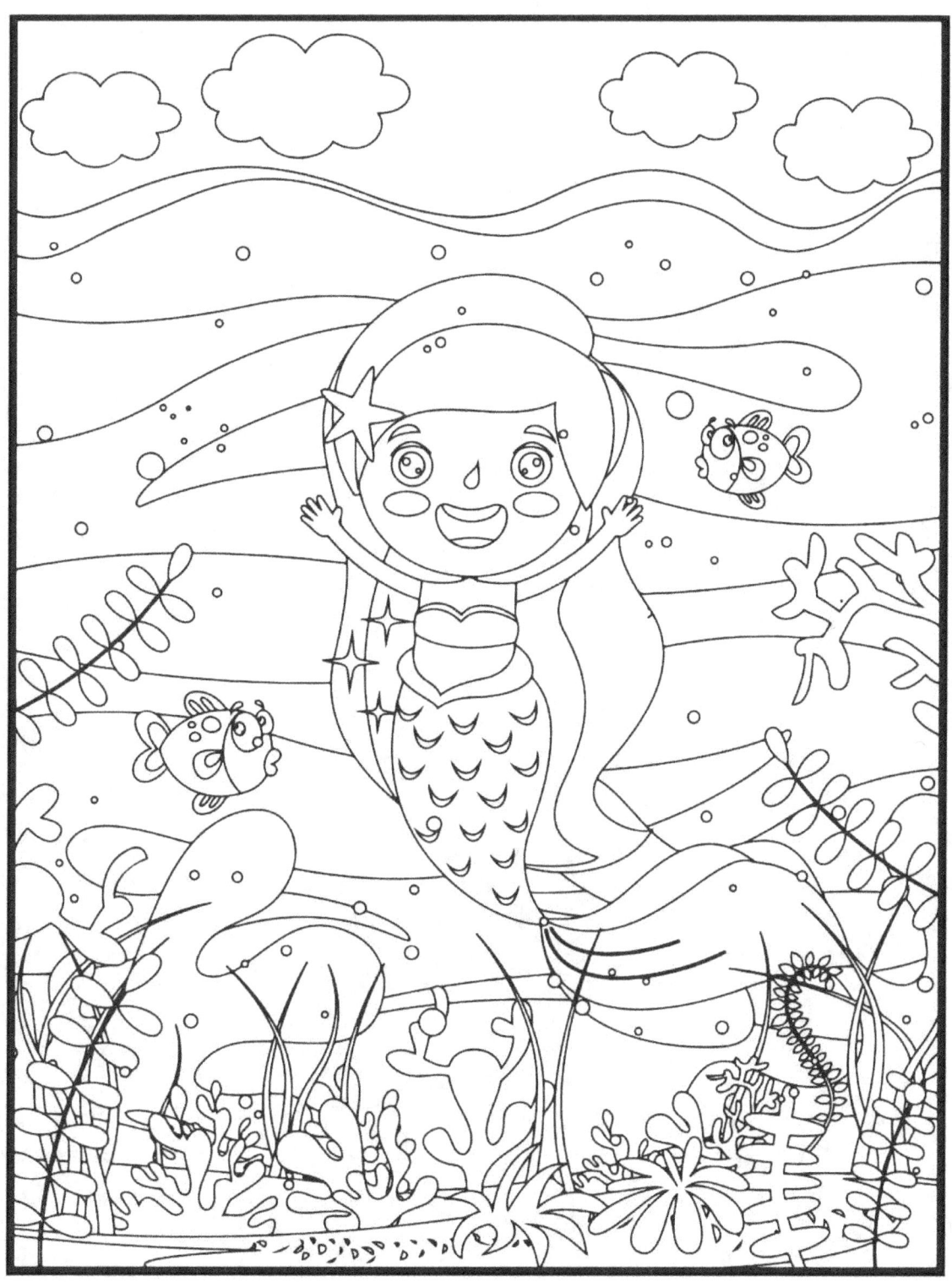

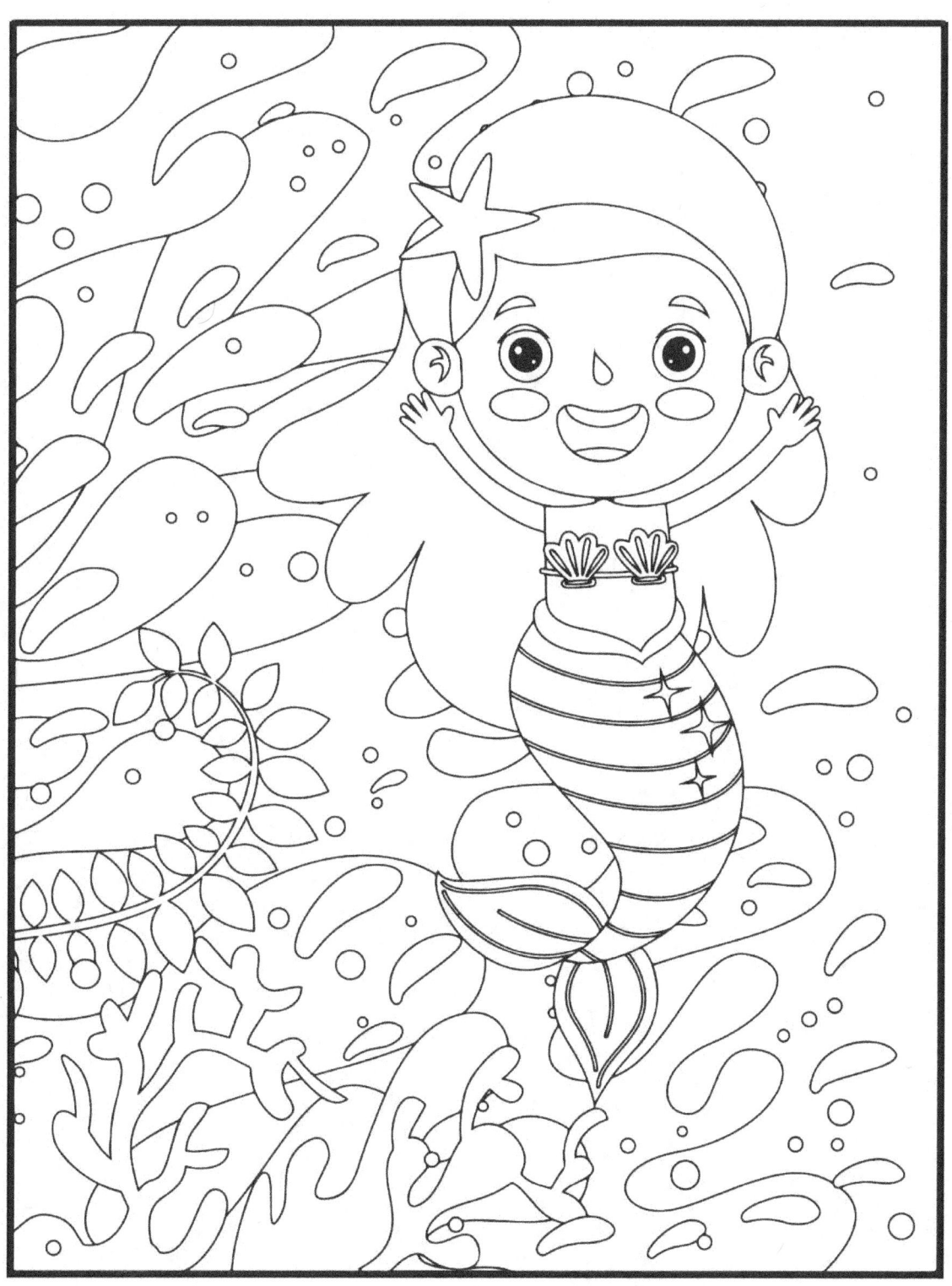

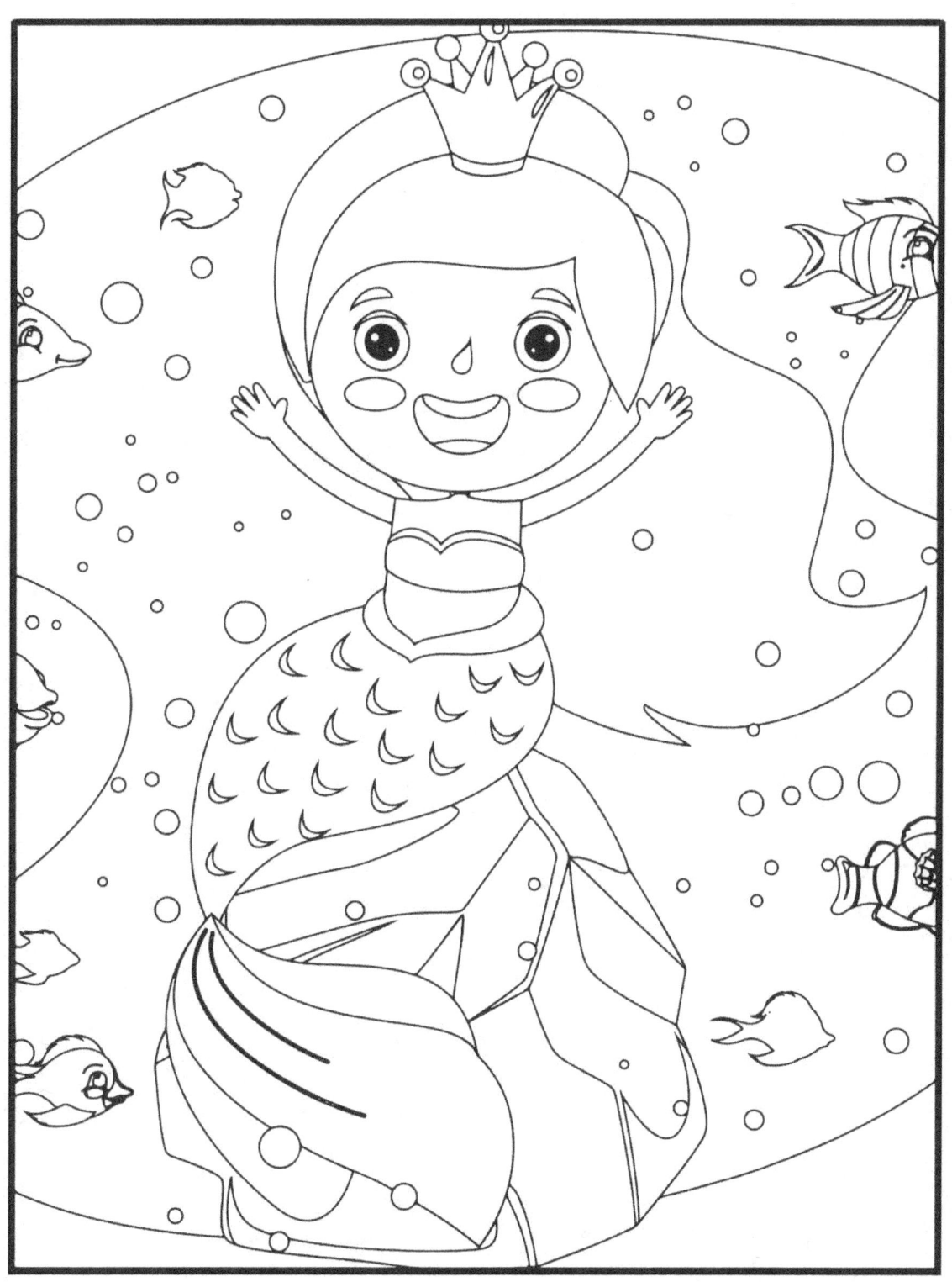

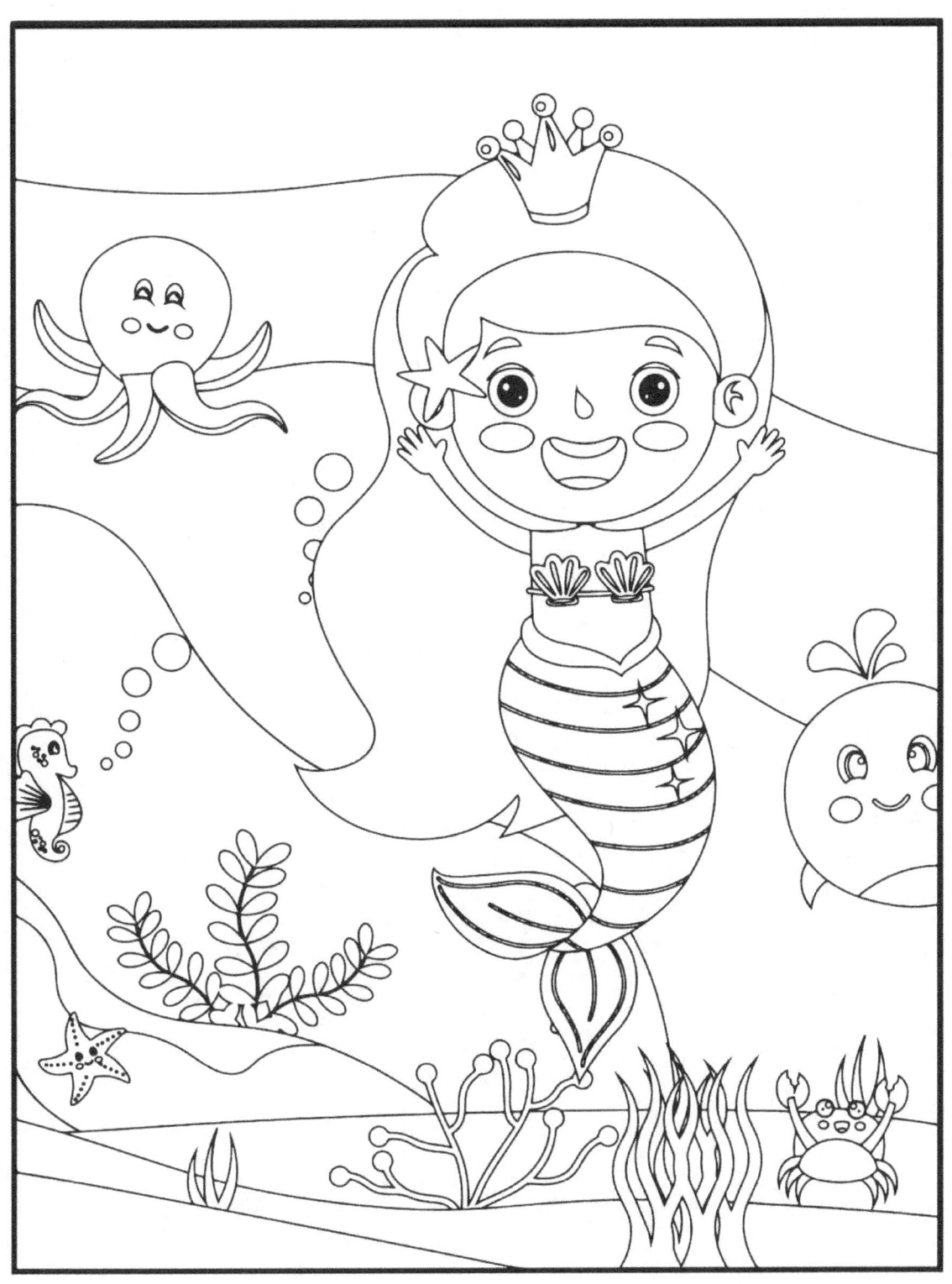

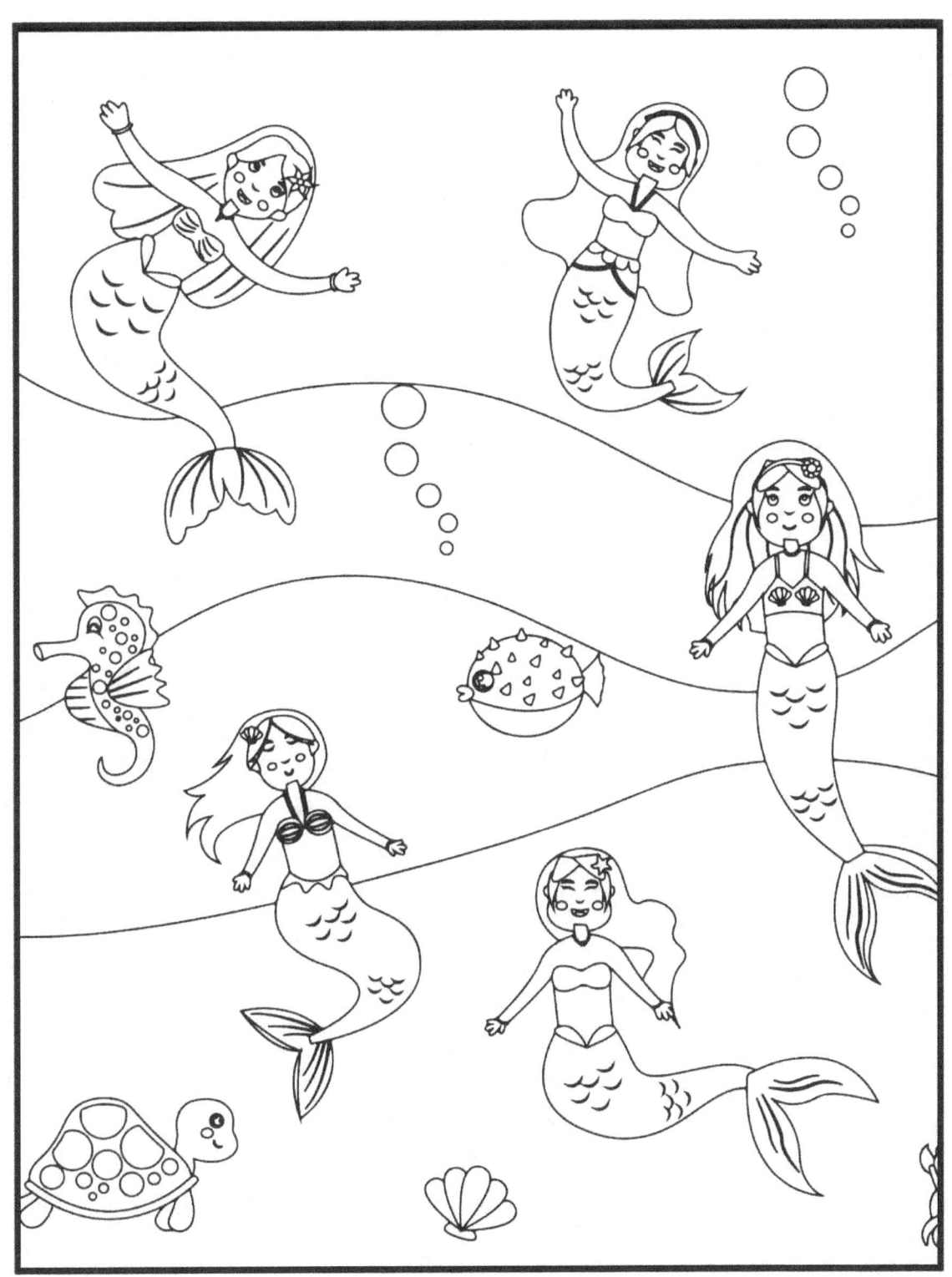

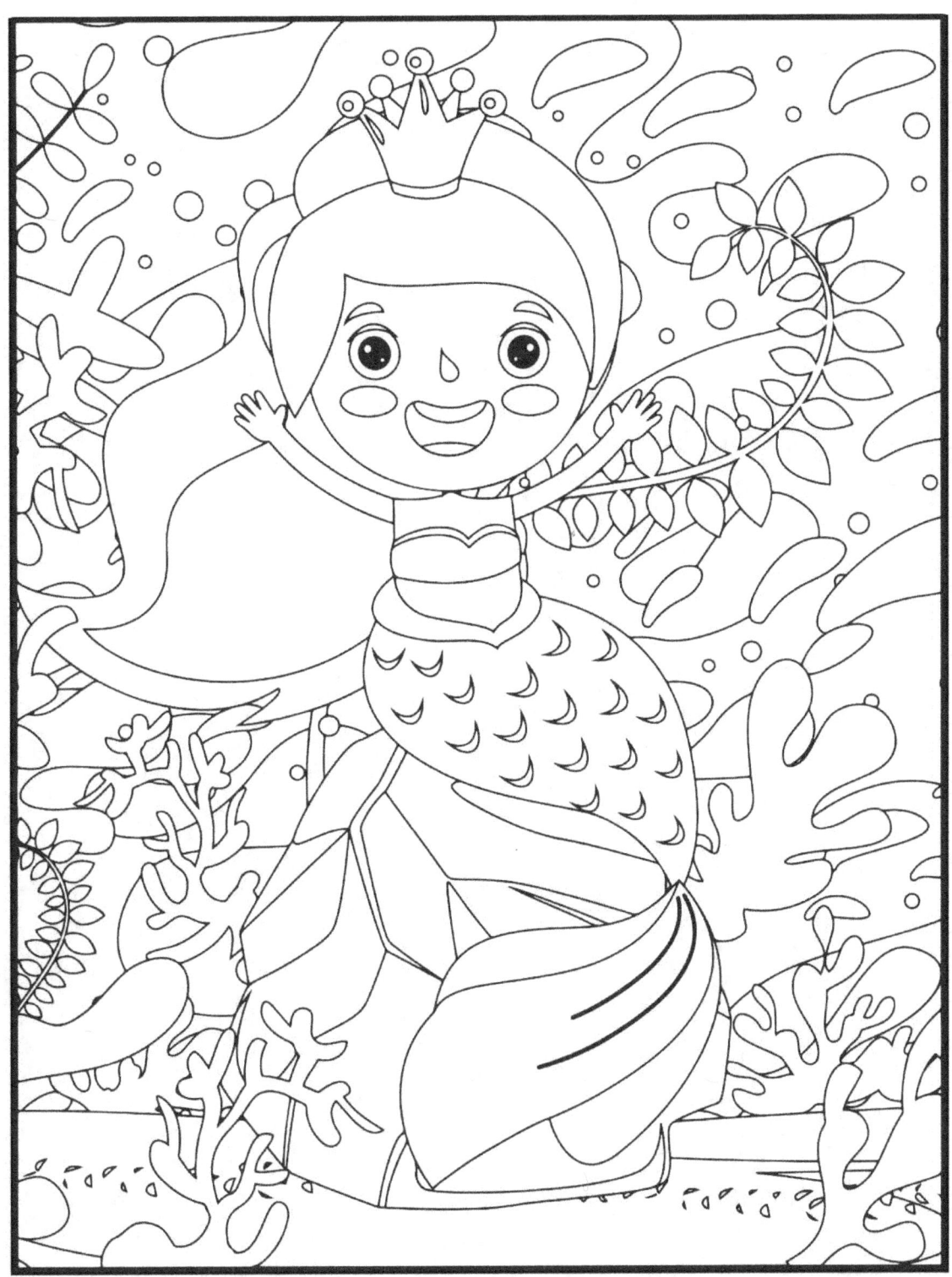

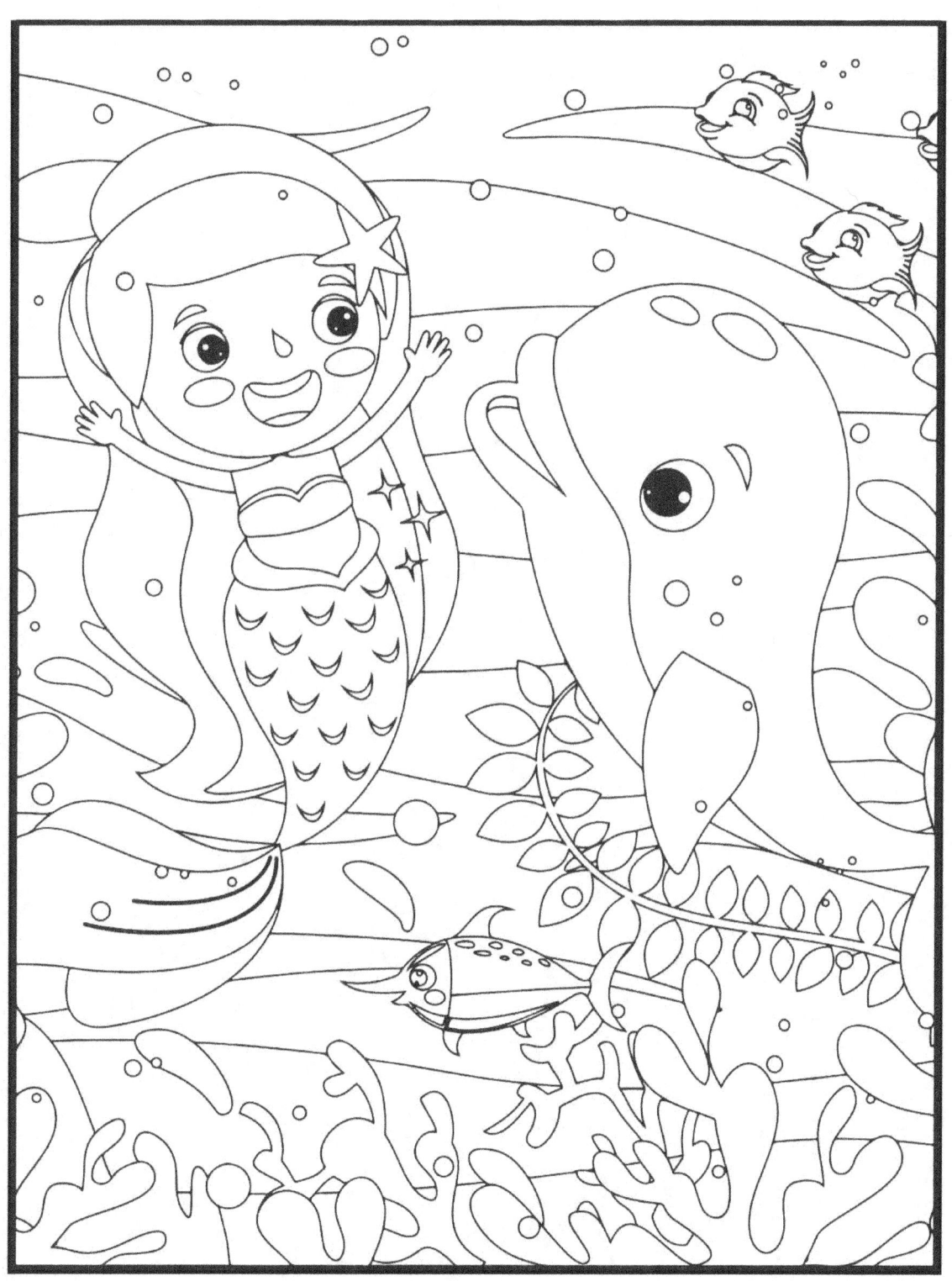

The Dot Game

Take turns connecting the dots until you make a square. Put your initials in each square. At the end, the person with the most squares win.

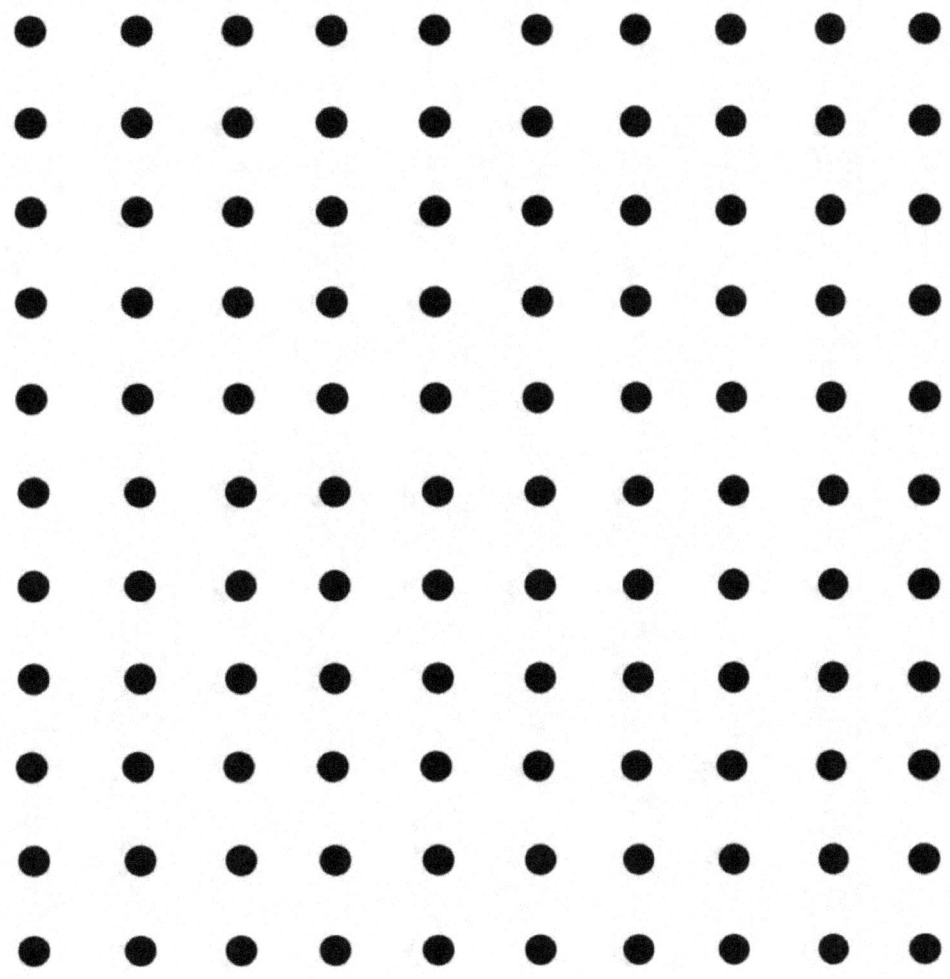

The Dot Game

Take turns connecting the dots until you make a square. Put your initials in each square. At the end, the person with the most squares win.

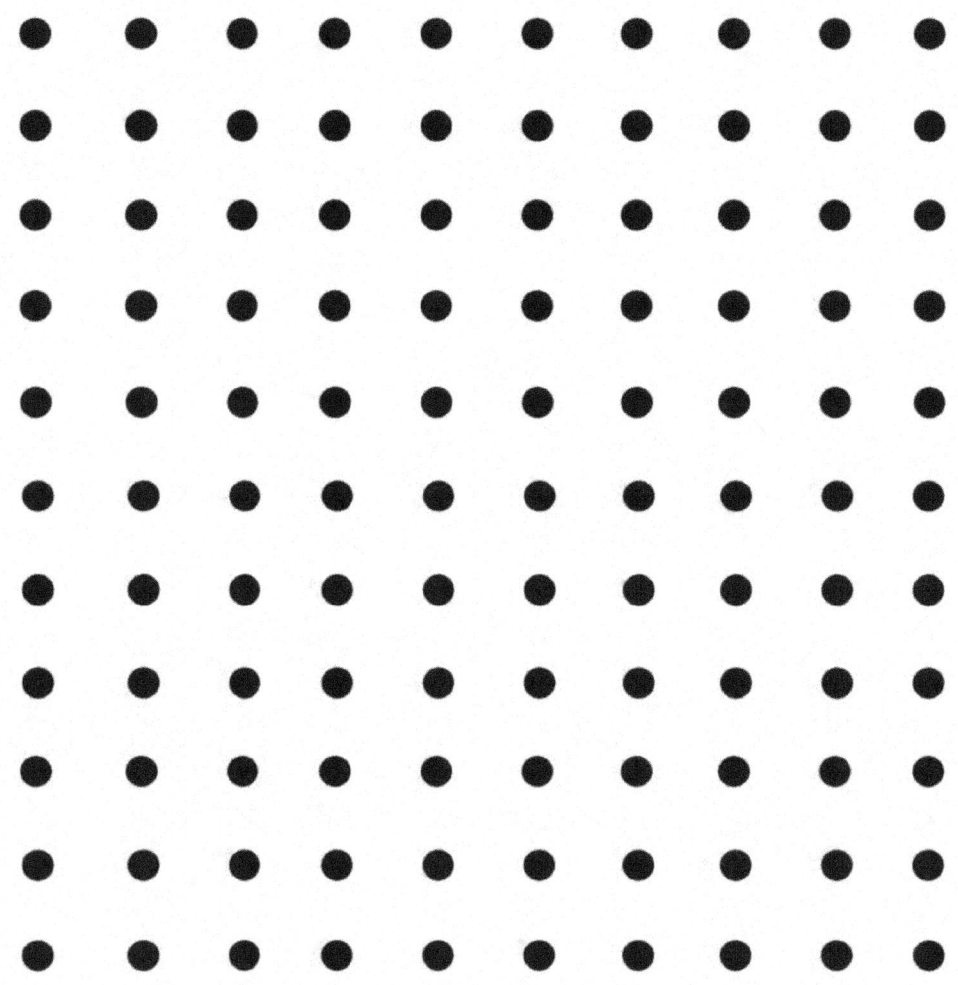

The Dot Game

Take turns connecting the dots until you make a square. Put your initials in each square. At the end, the person with the most squares win.

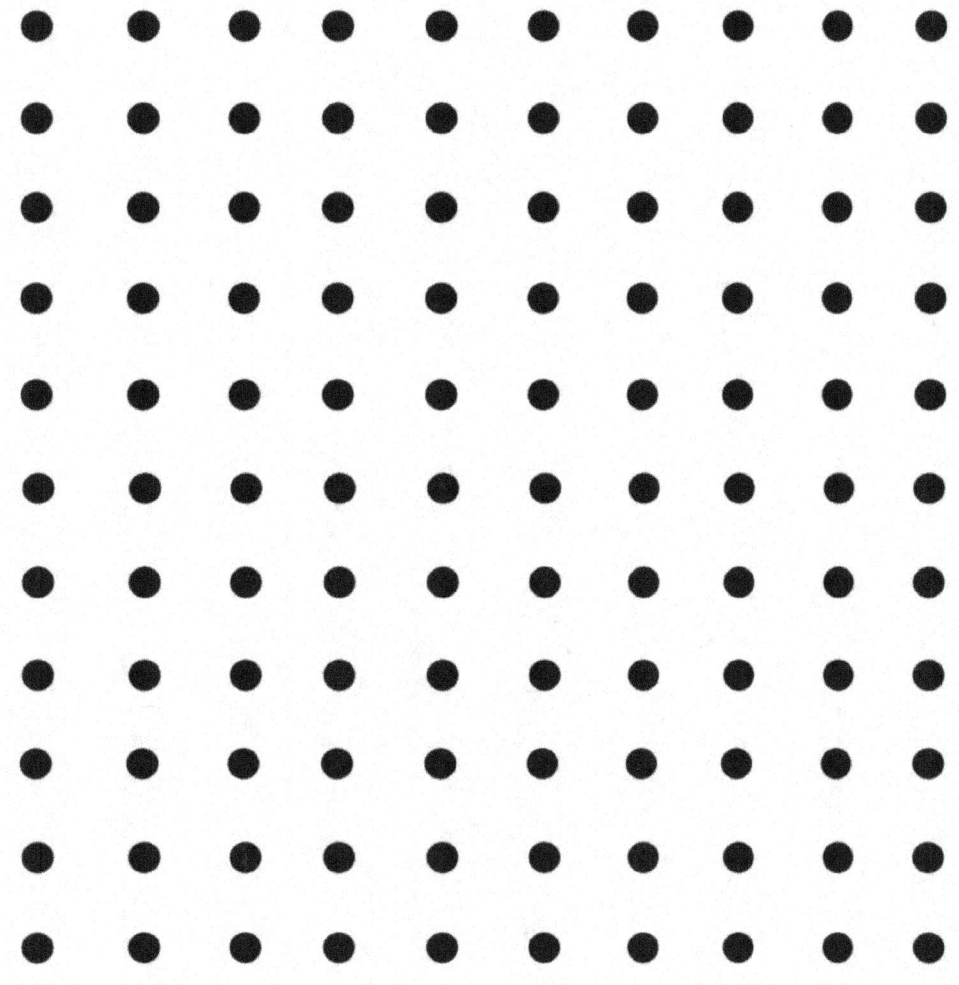

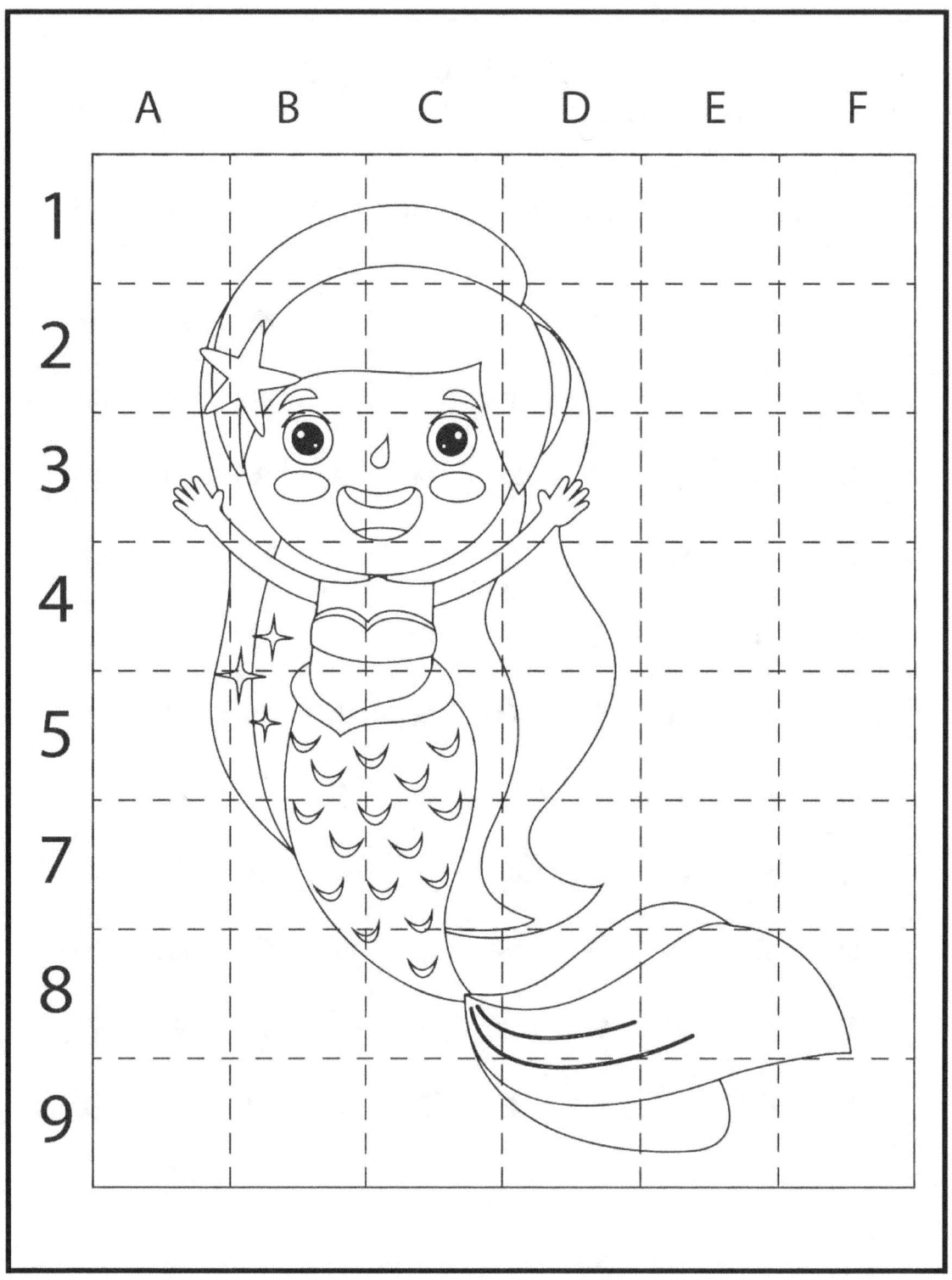

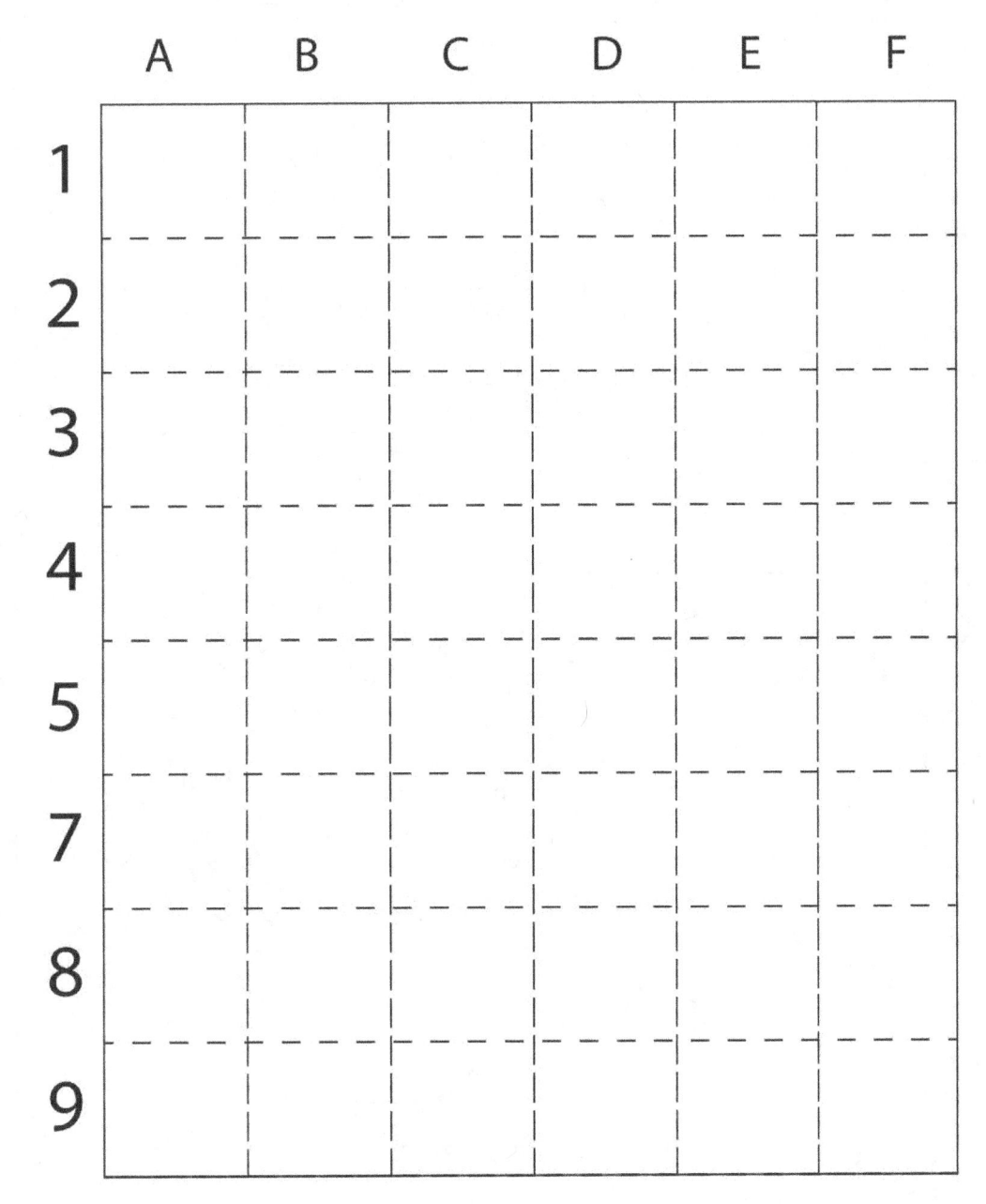

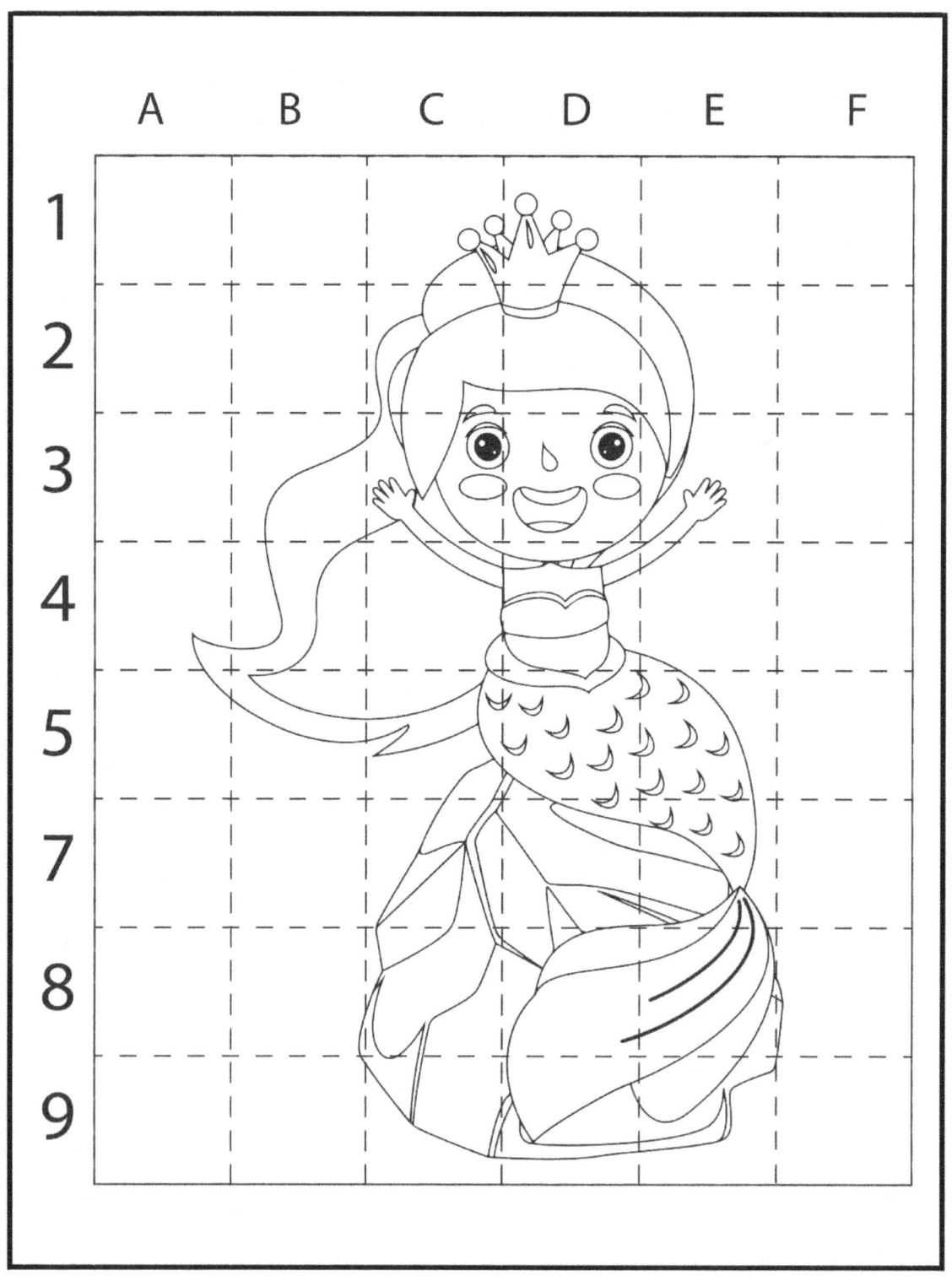

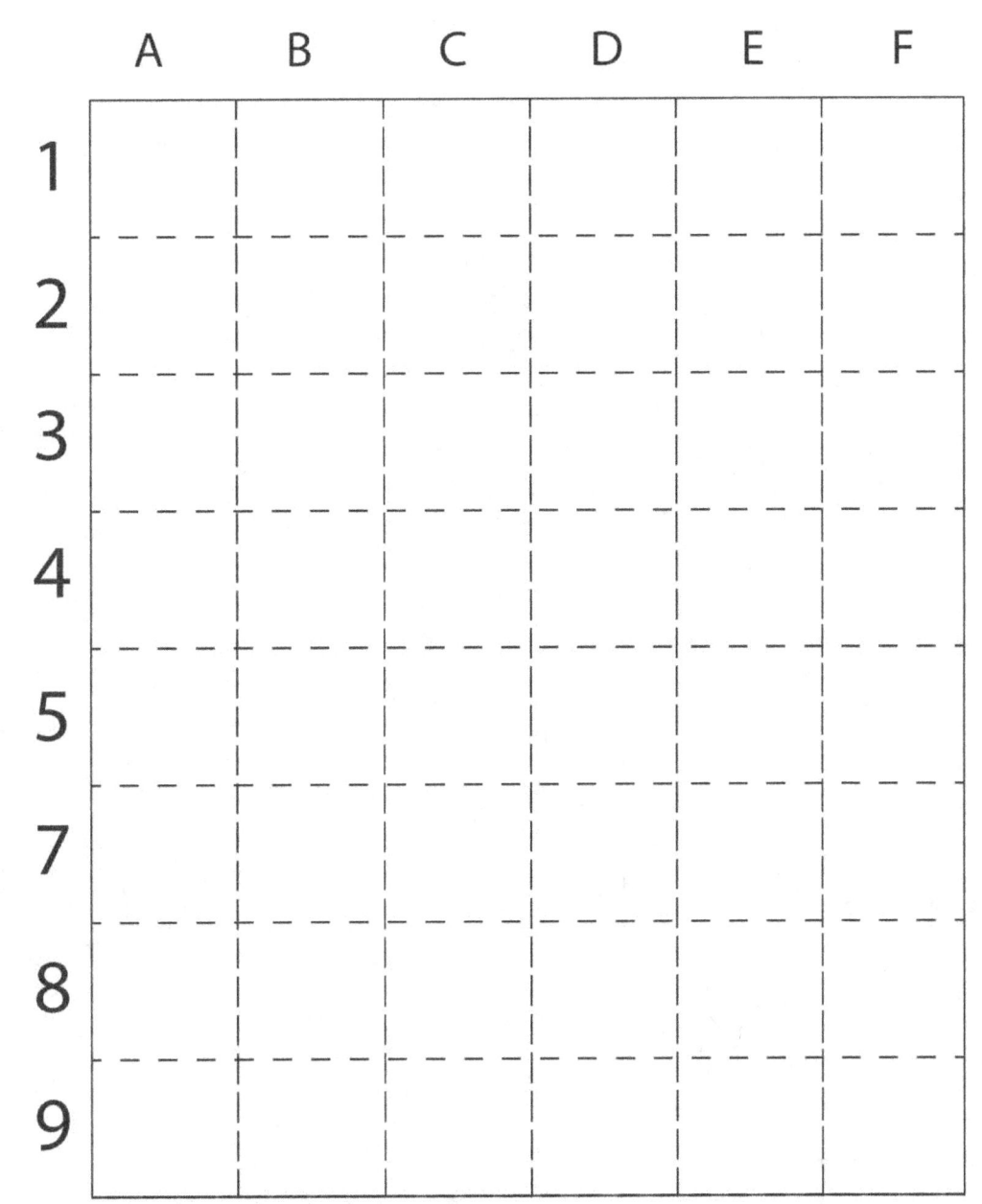

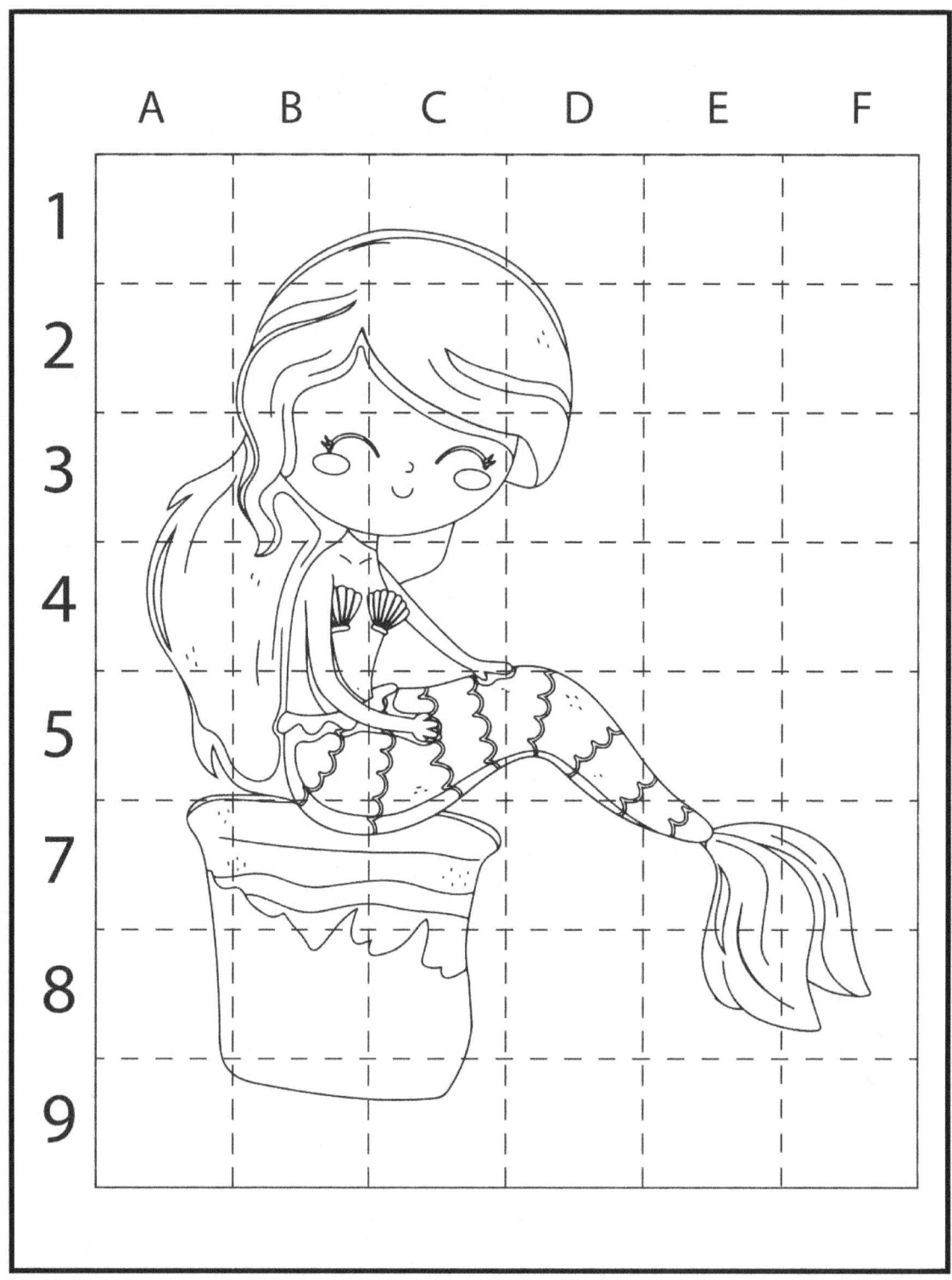

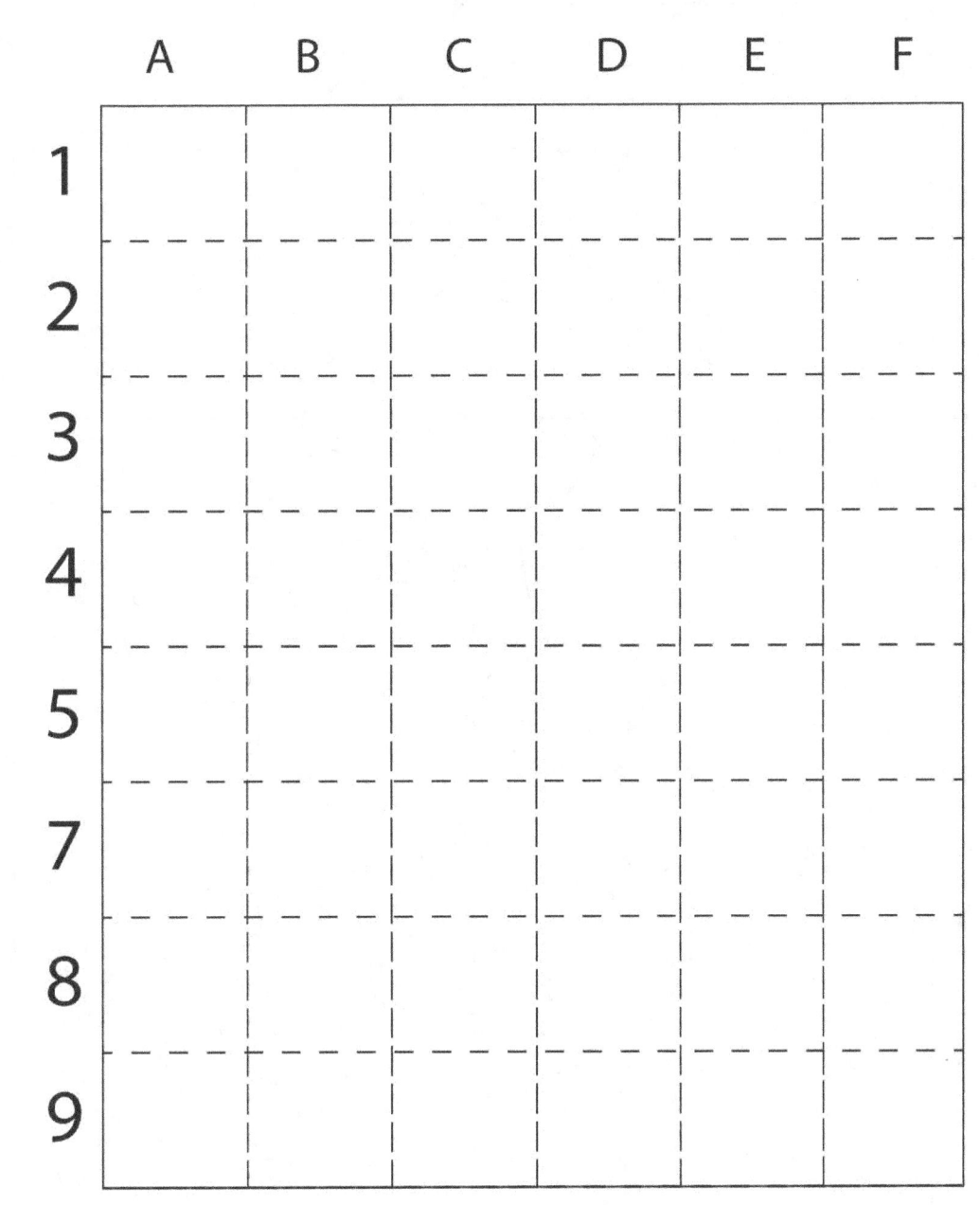

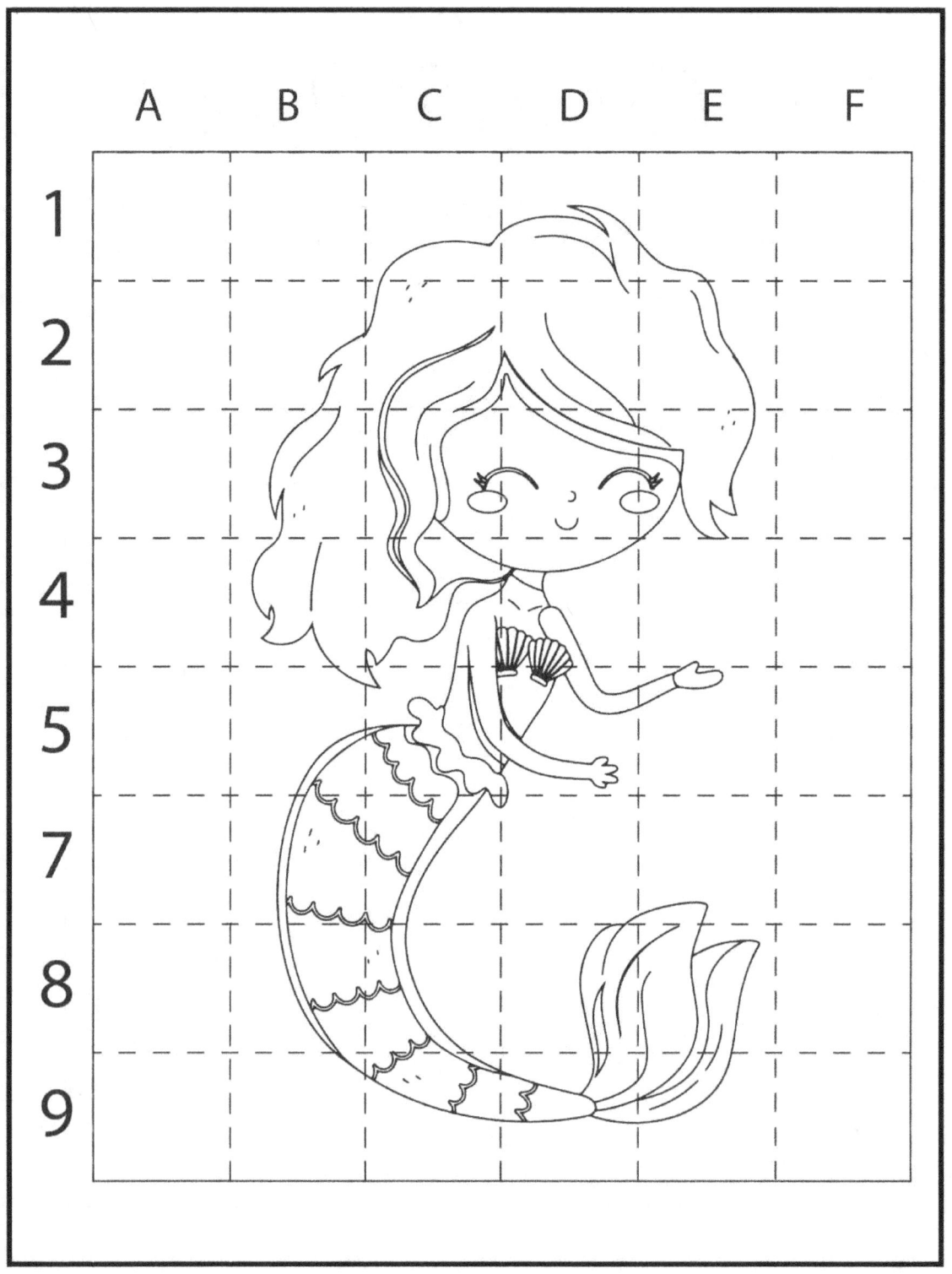

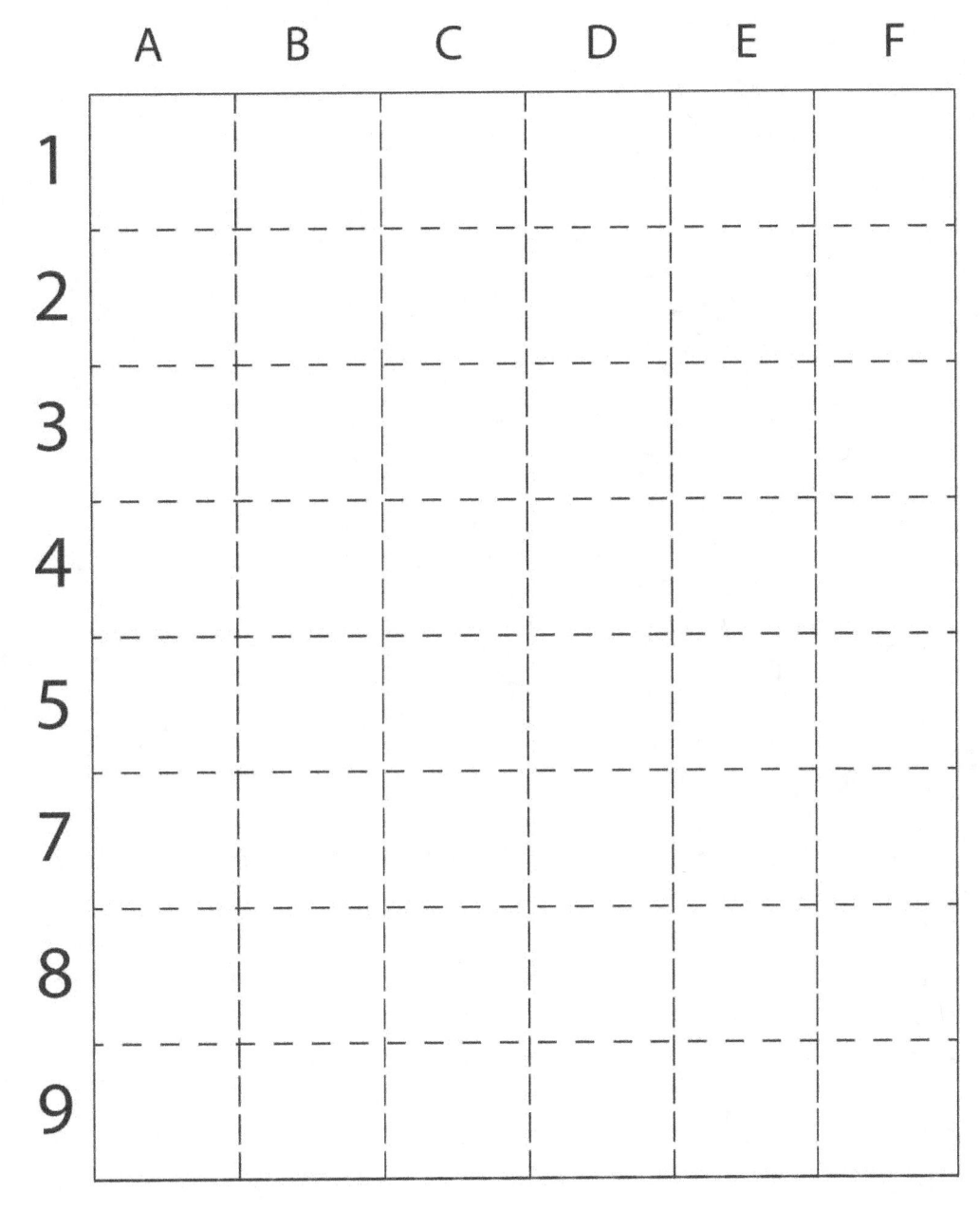

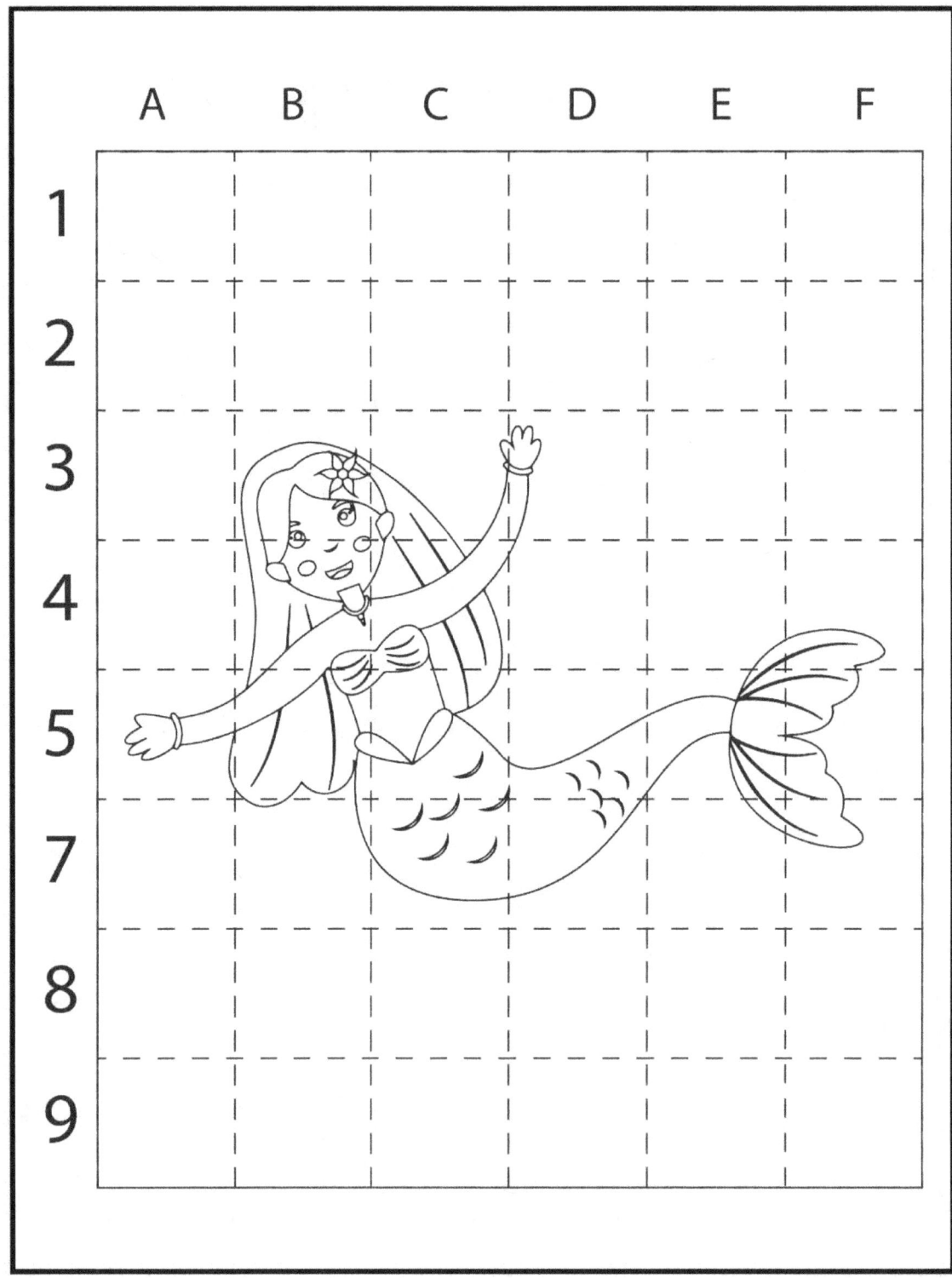

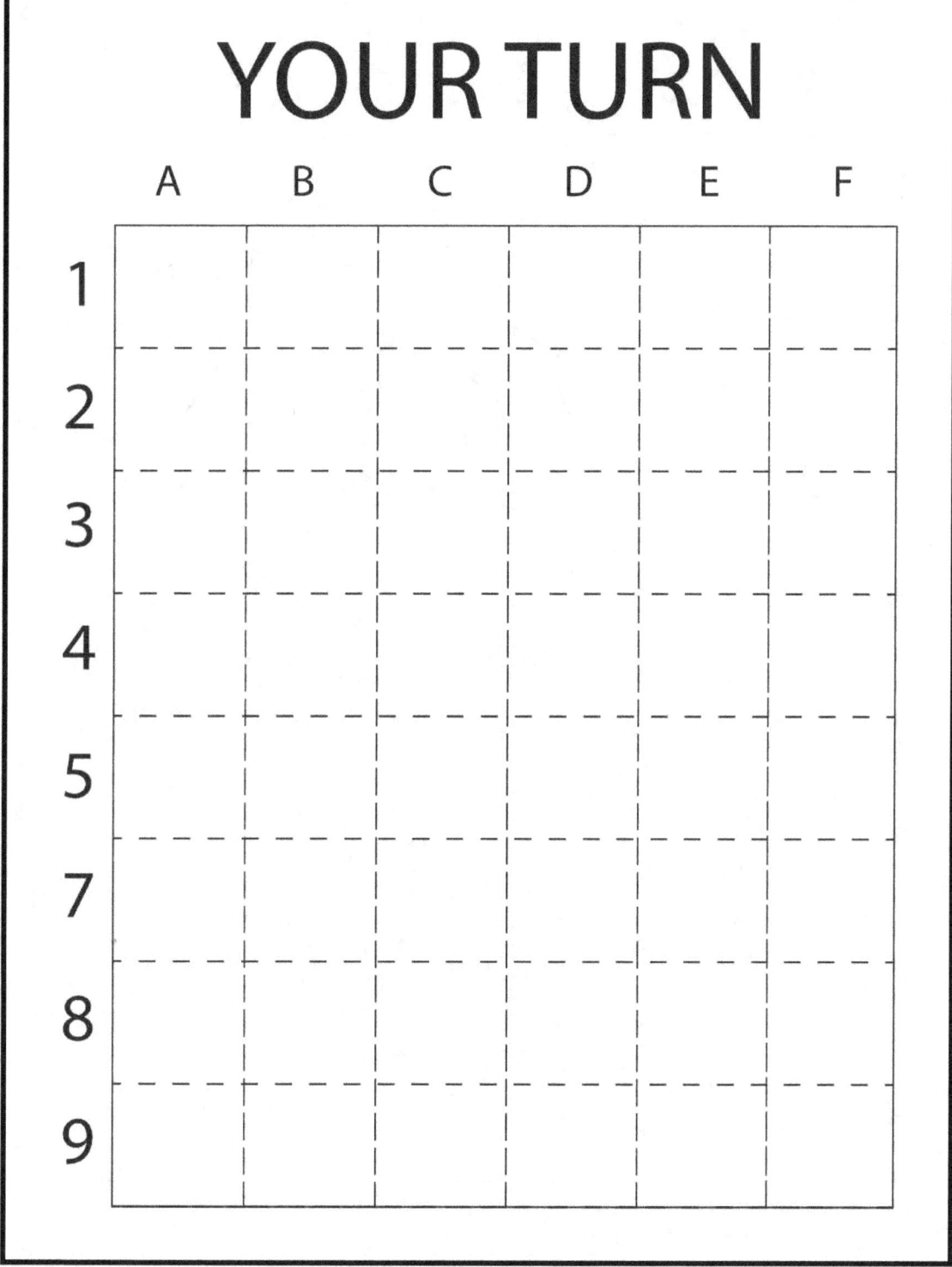

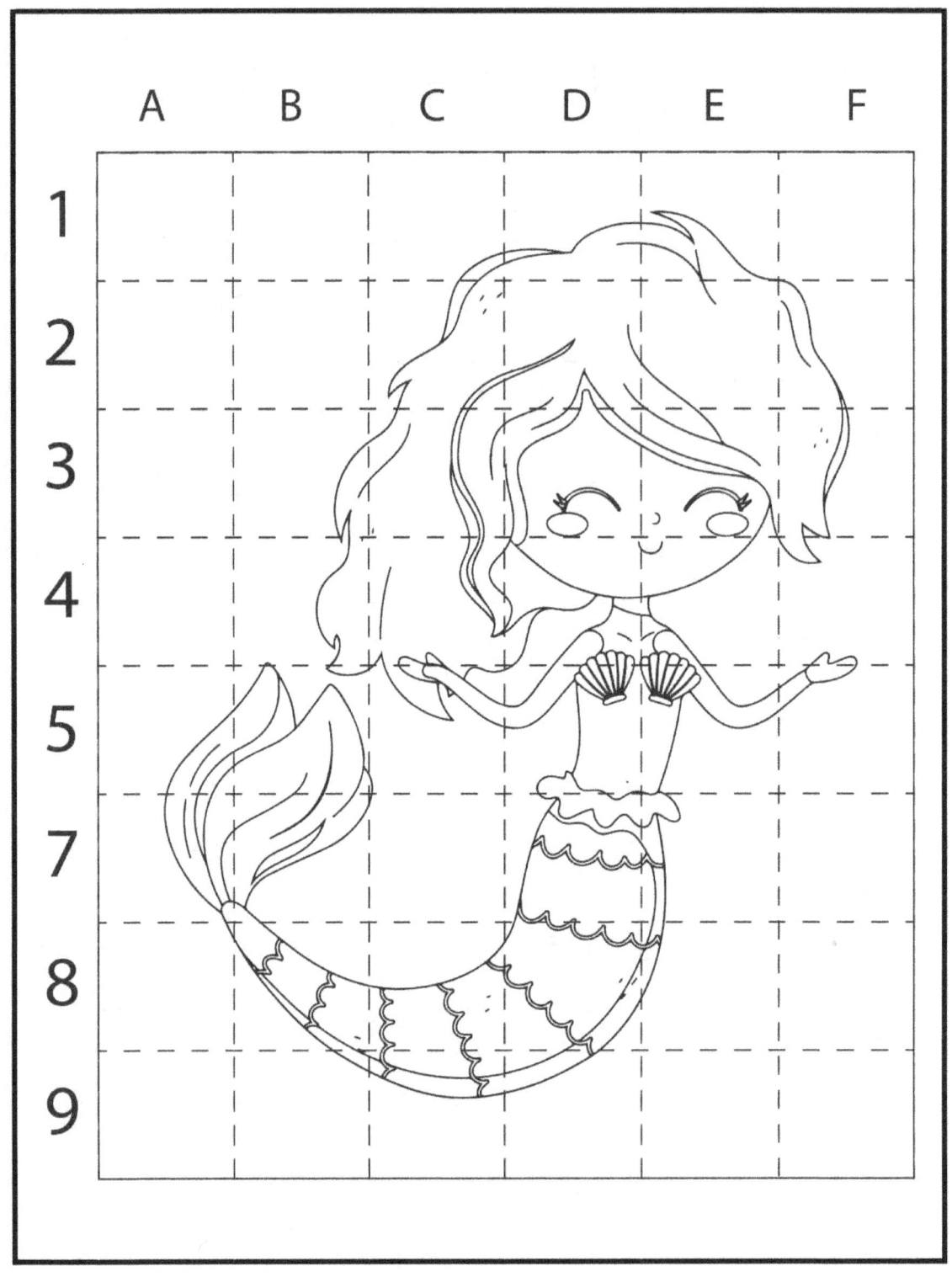

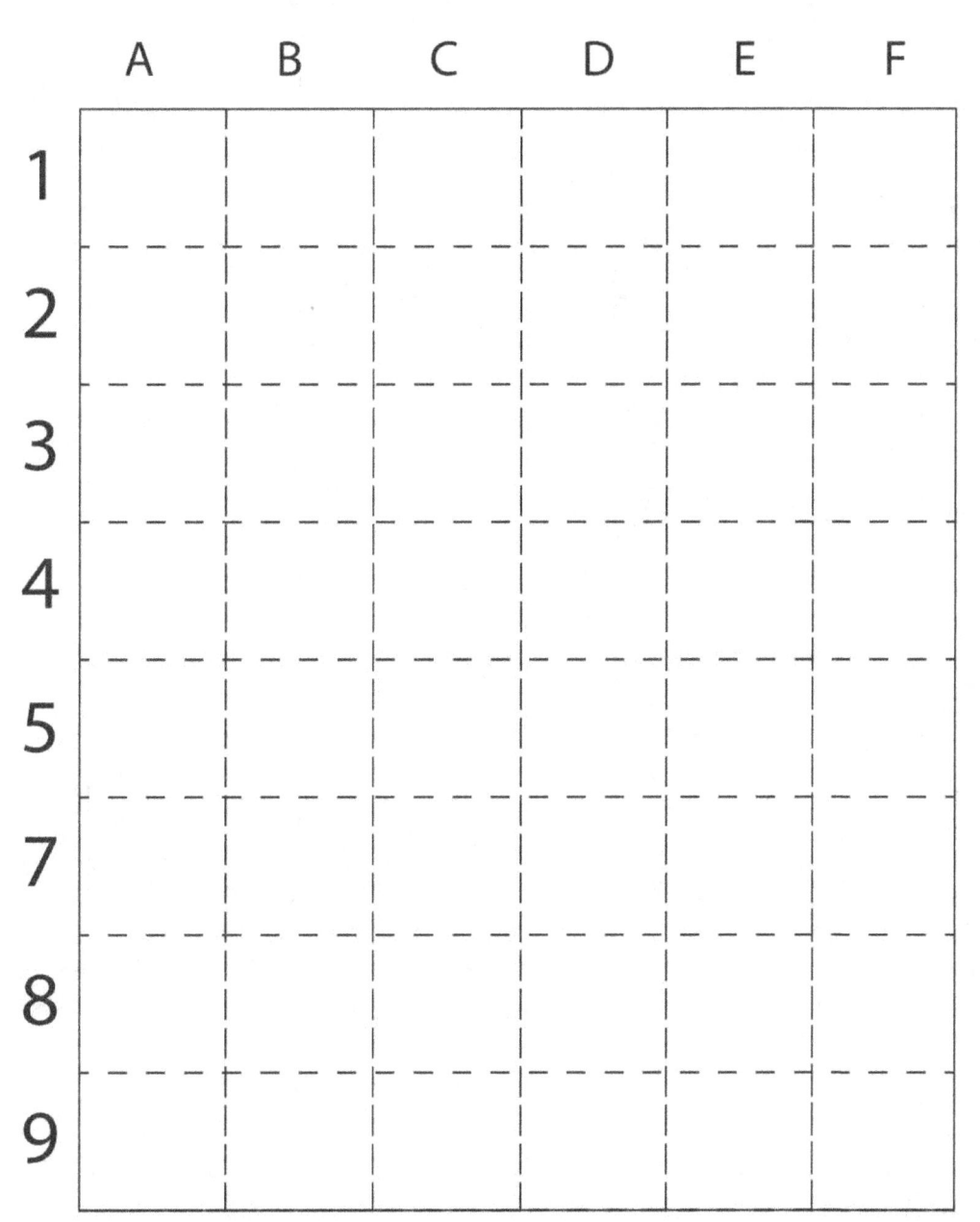

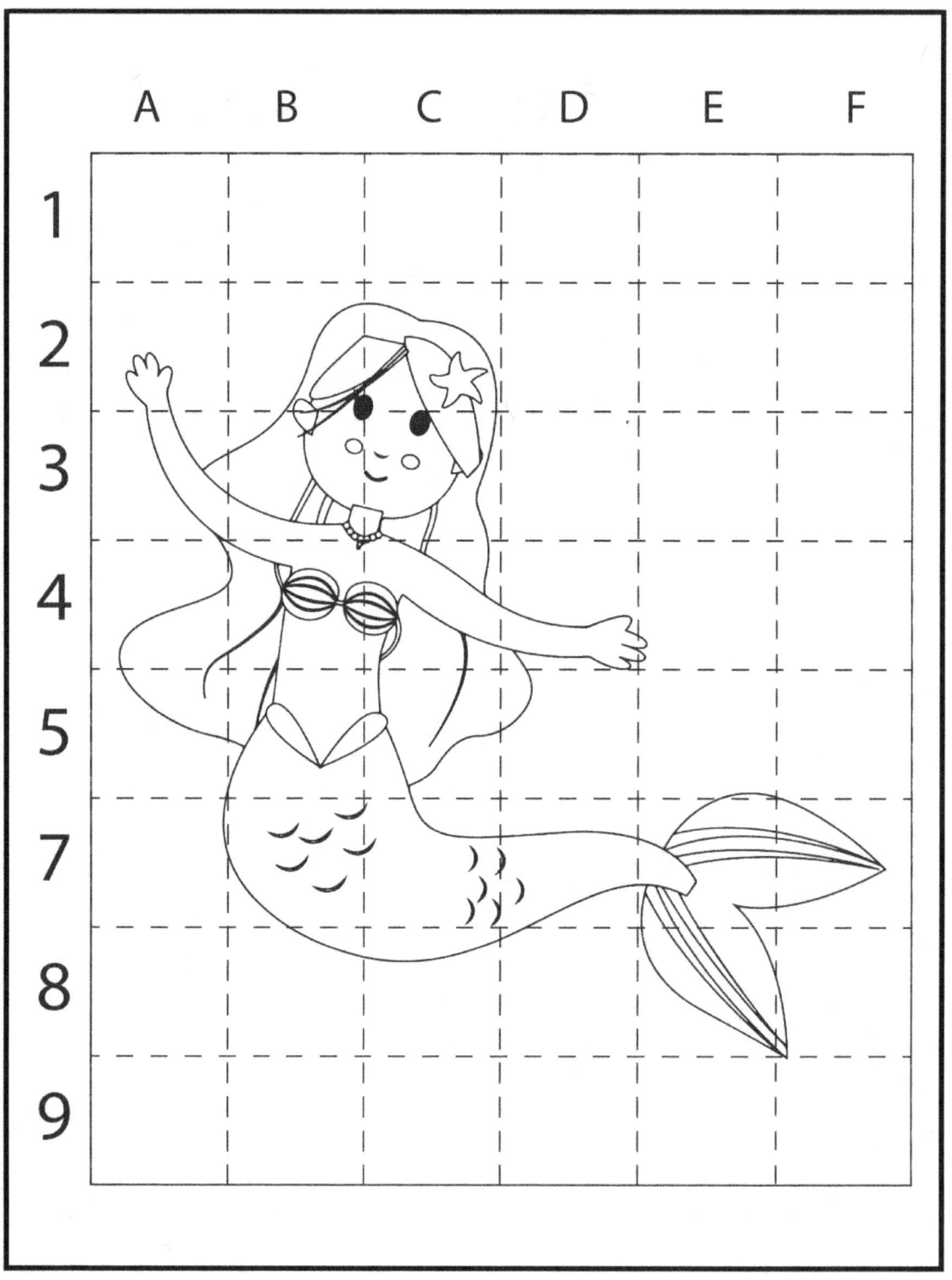

YOUR TURN

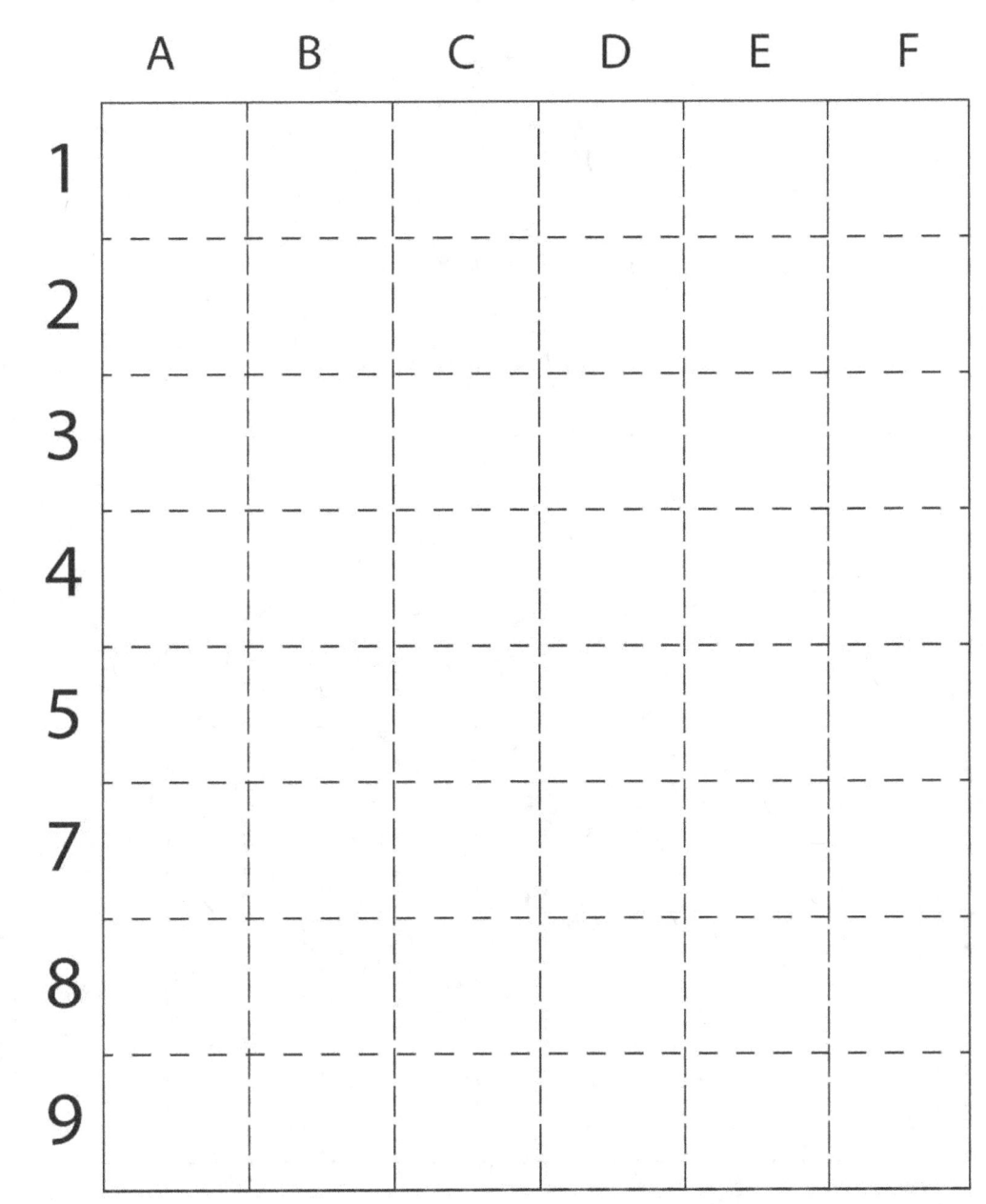

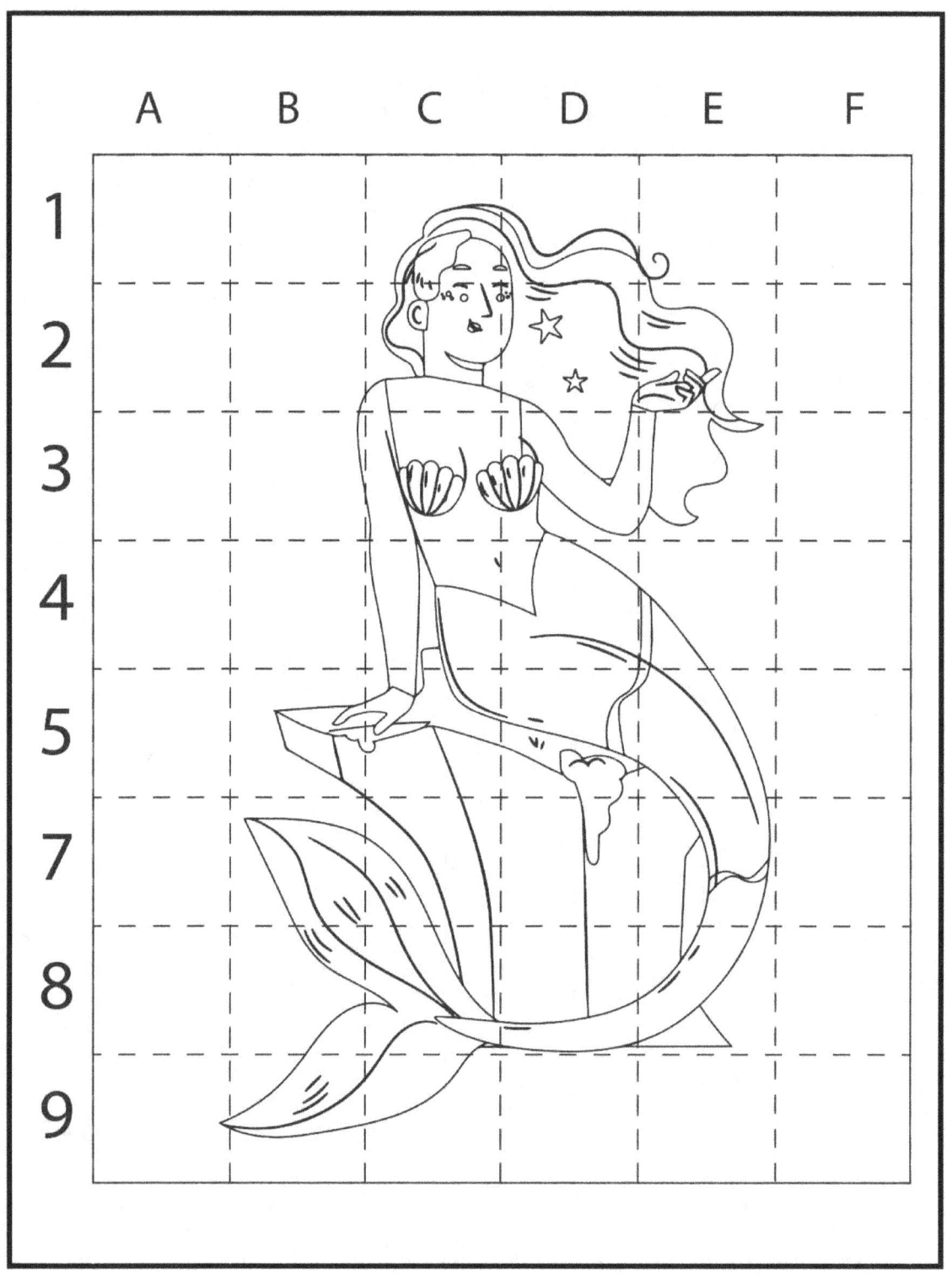

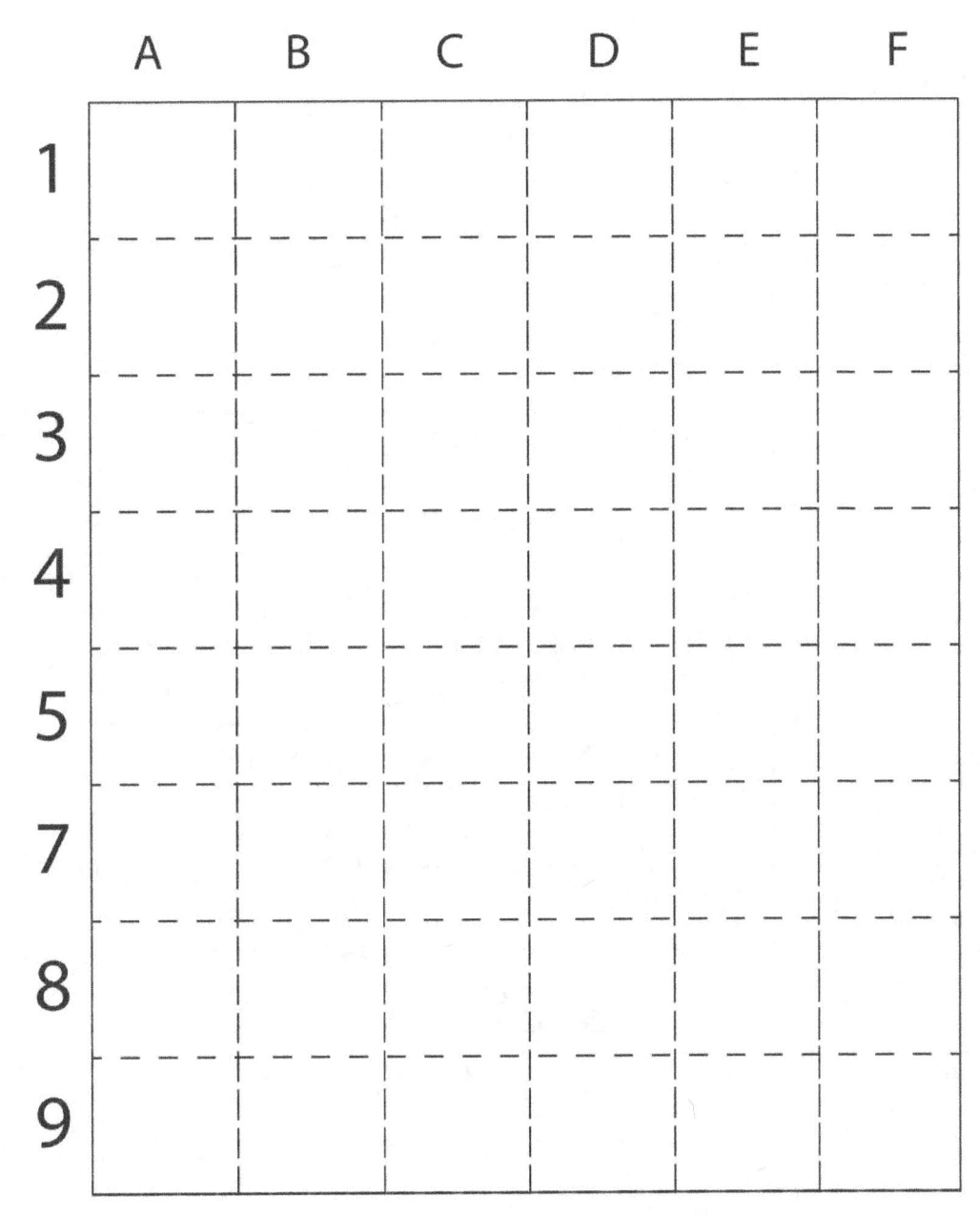

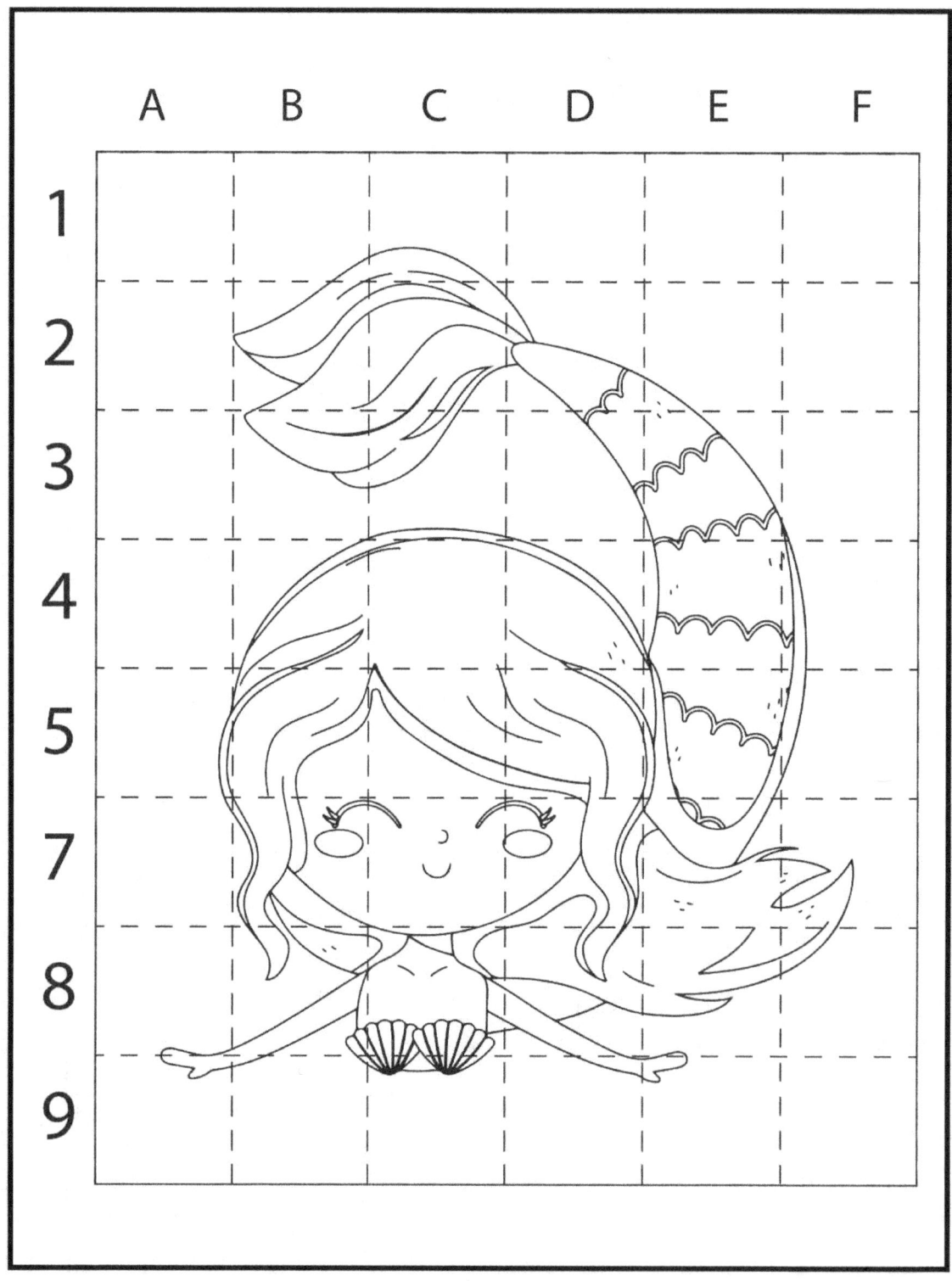

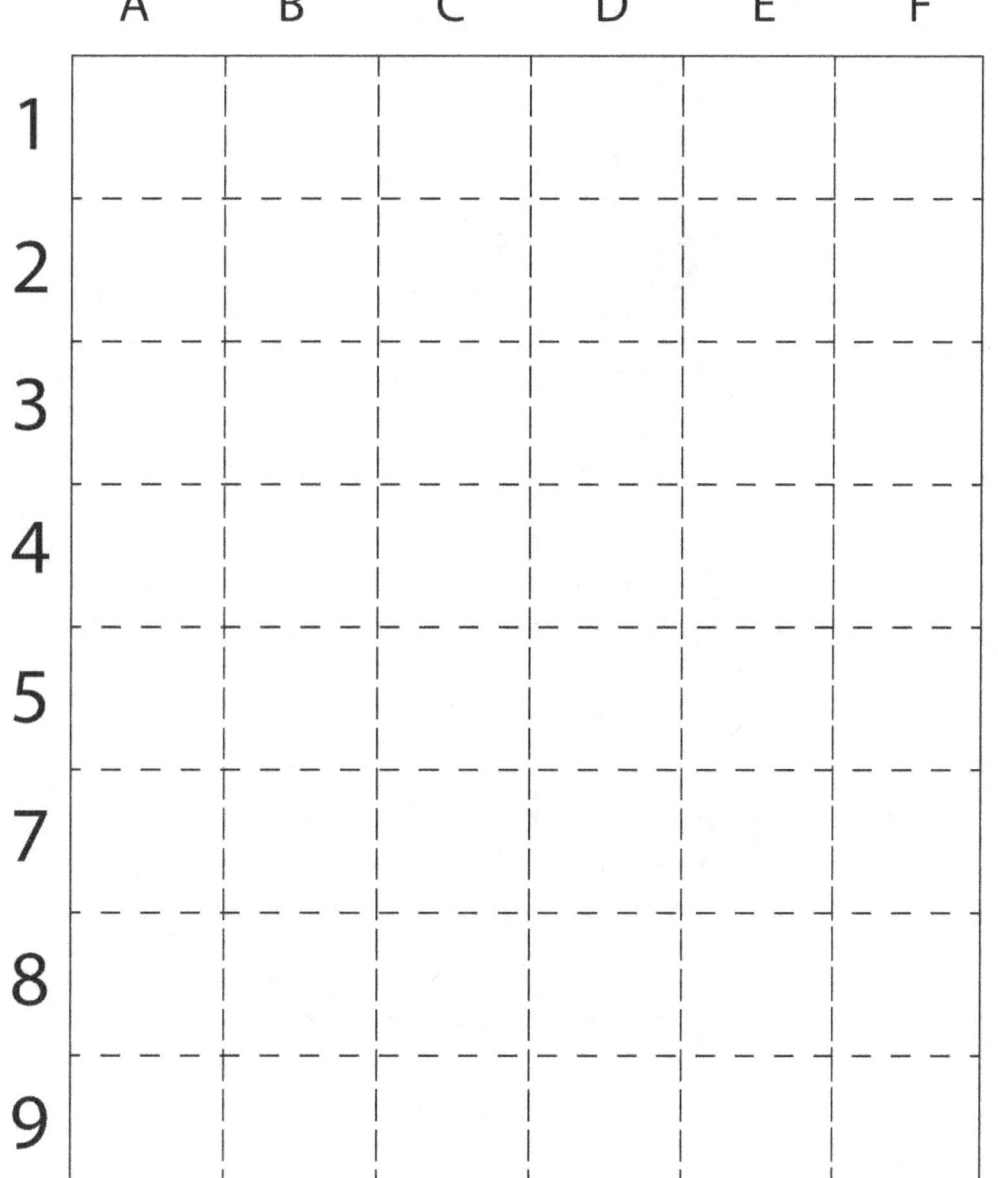

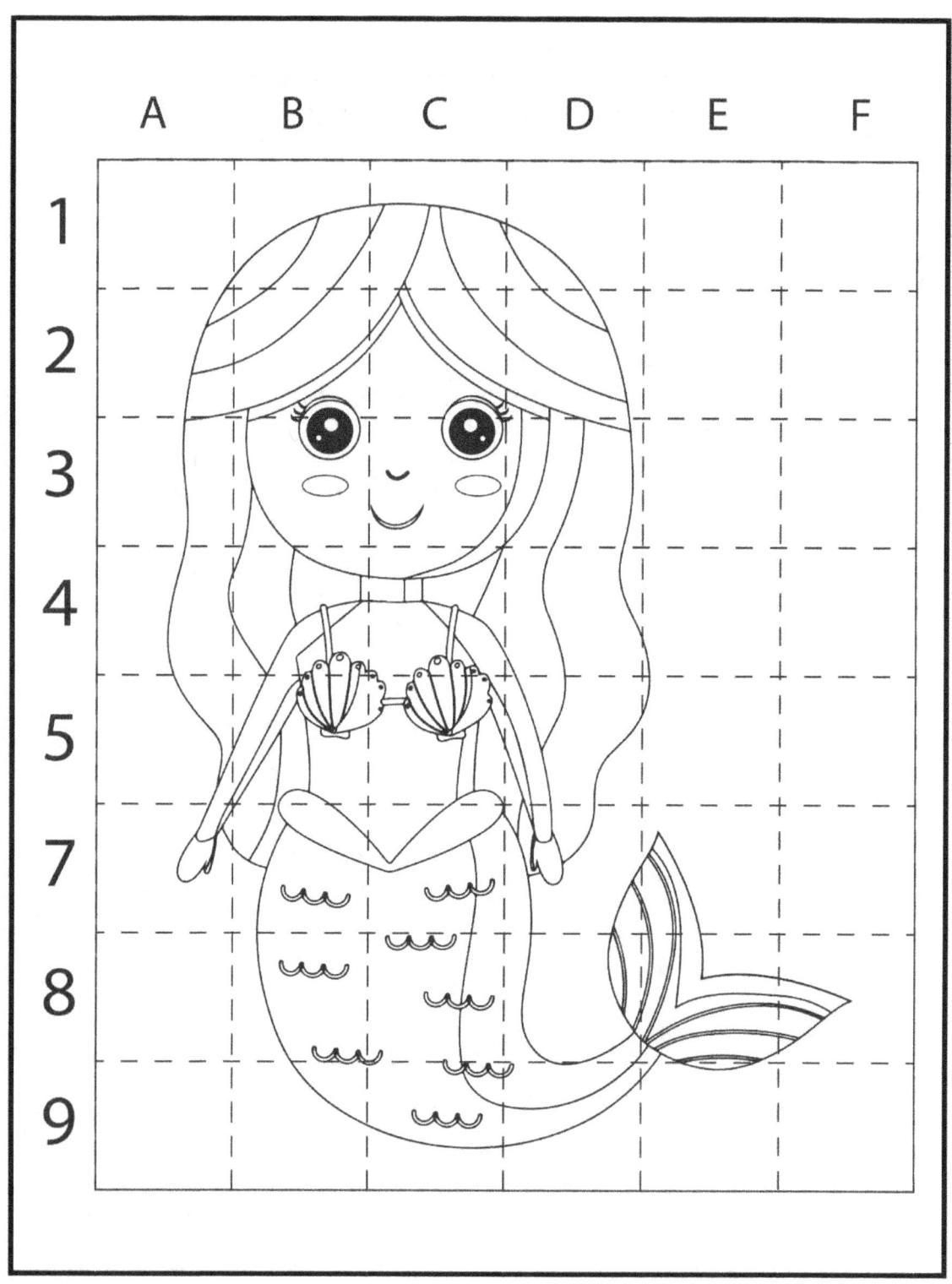

YOUR TURN

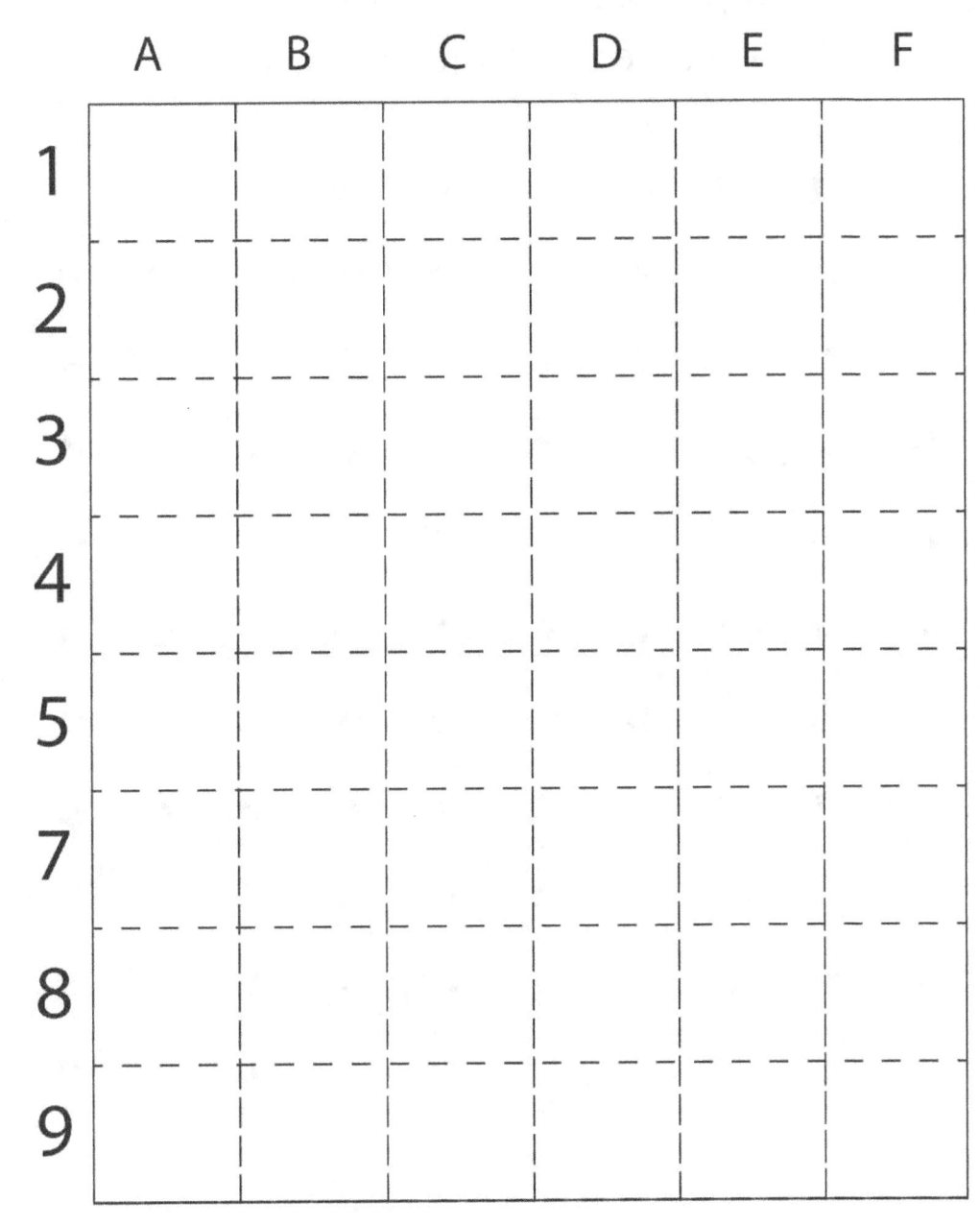

The Dot Game

Take turns connecting the dots until you make a square. Put your initials in each square. At the end, the person with the most squares win.

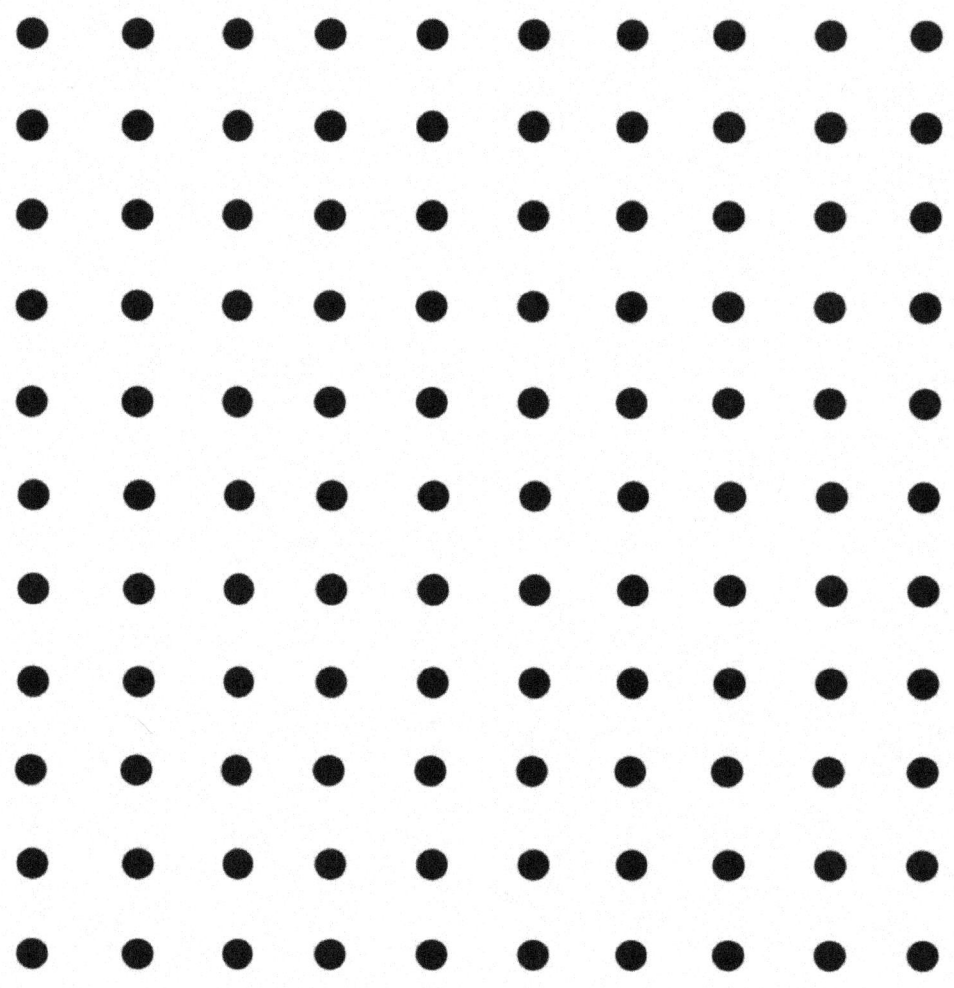

The Dot Game
Take turns connecting the dots until you make a square. Put your initials in each square. At the end, the person with the most squares win.

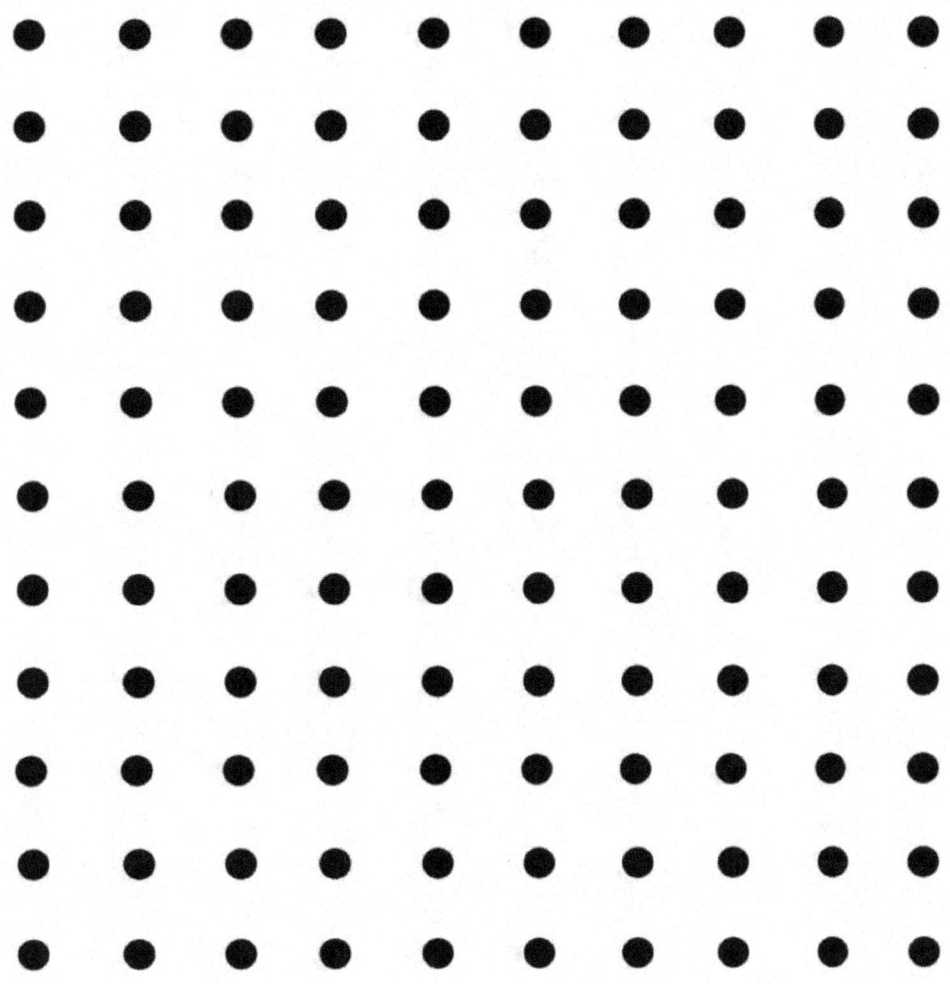

The Dot Game

Take turns connecting the dots until you make a square. Put your initials in each square. At the end, the person with the most squares win.

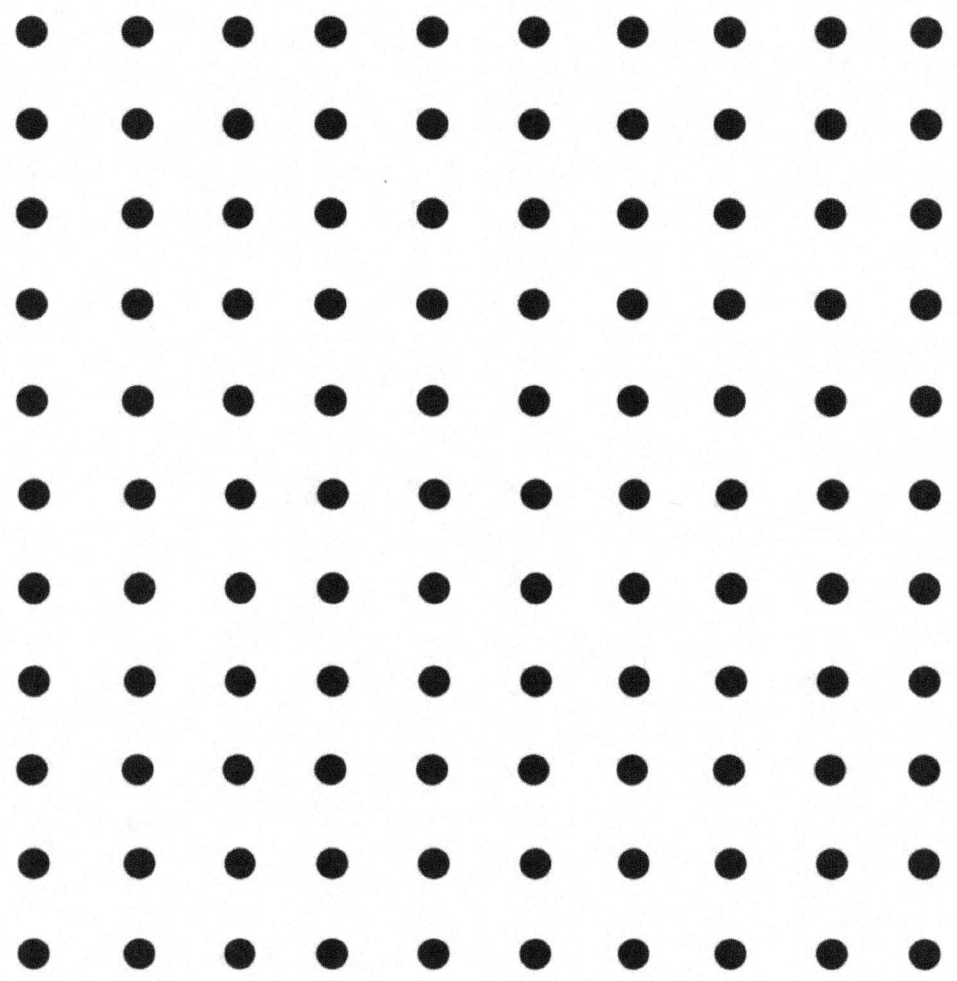

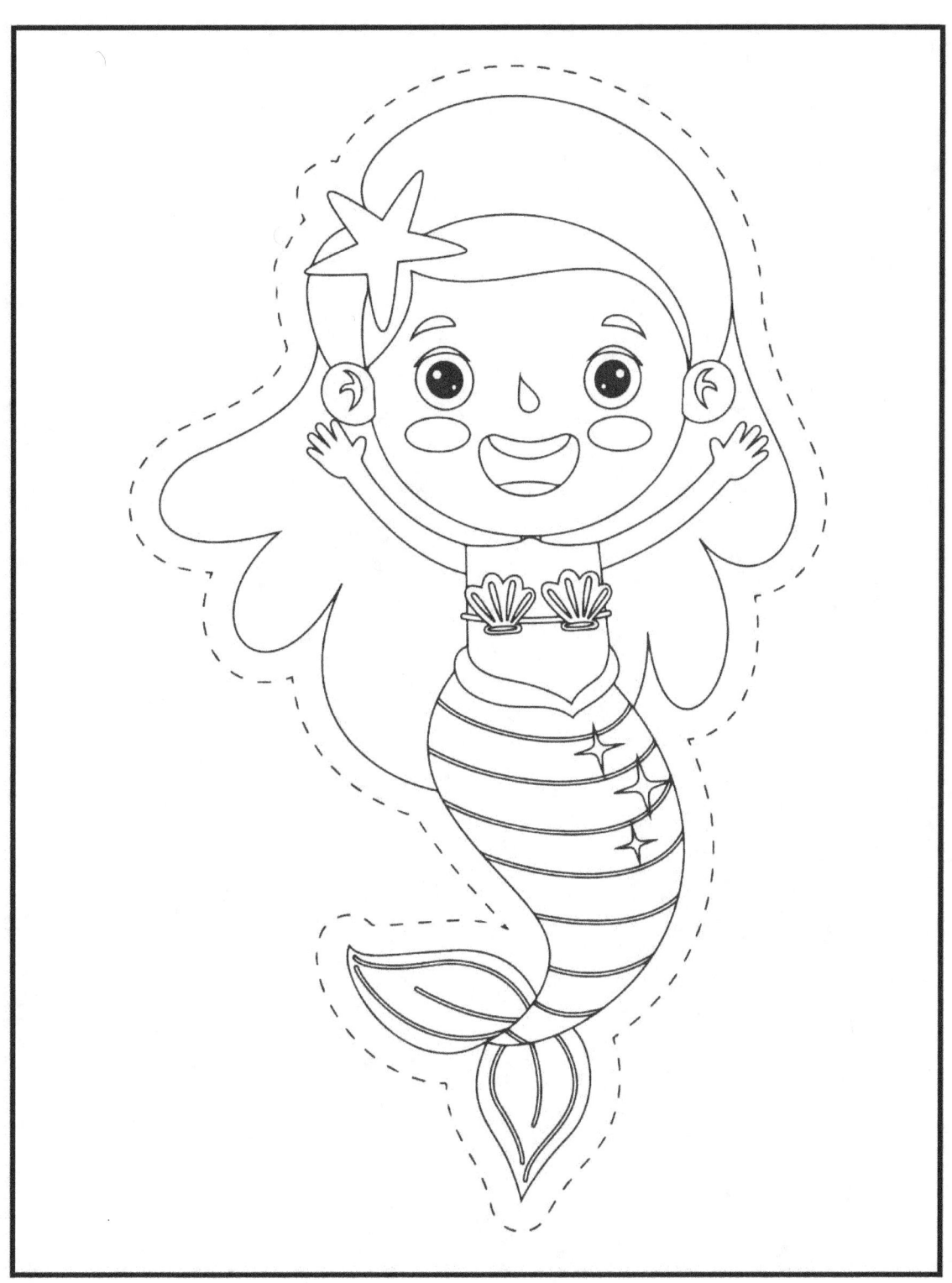

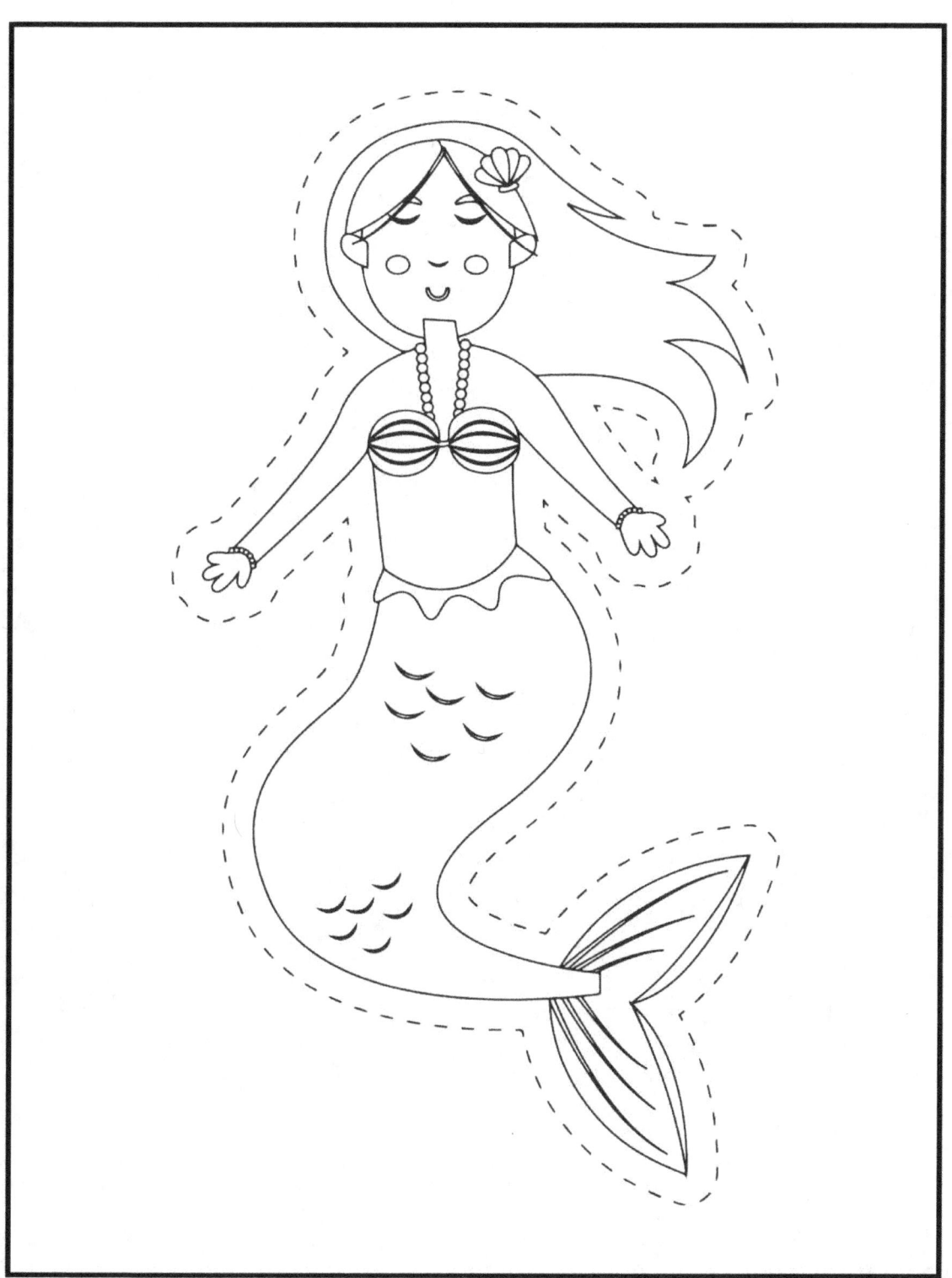

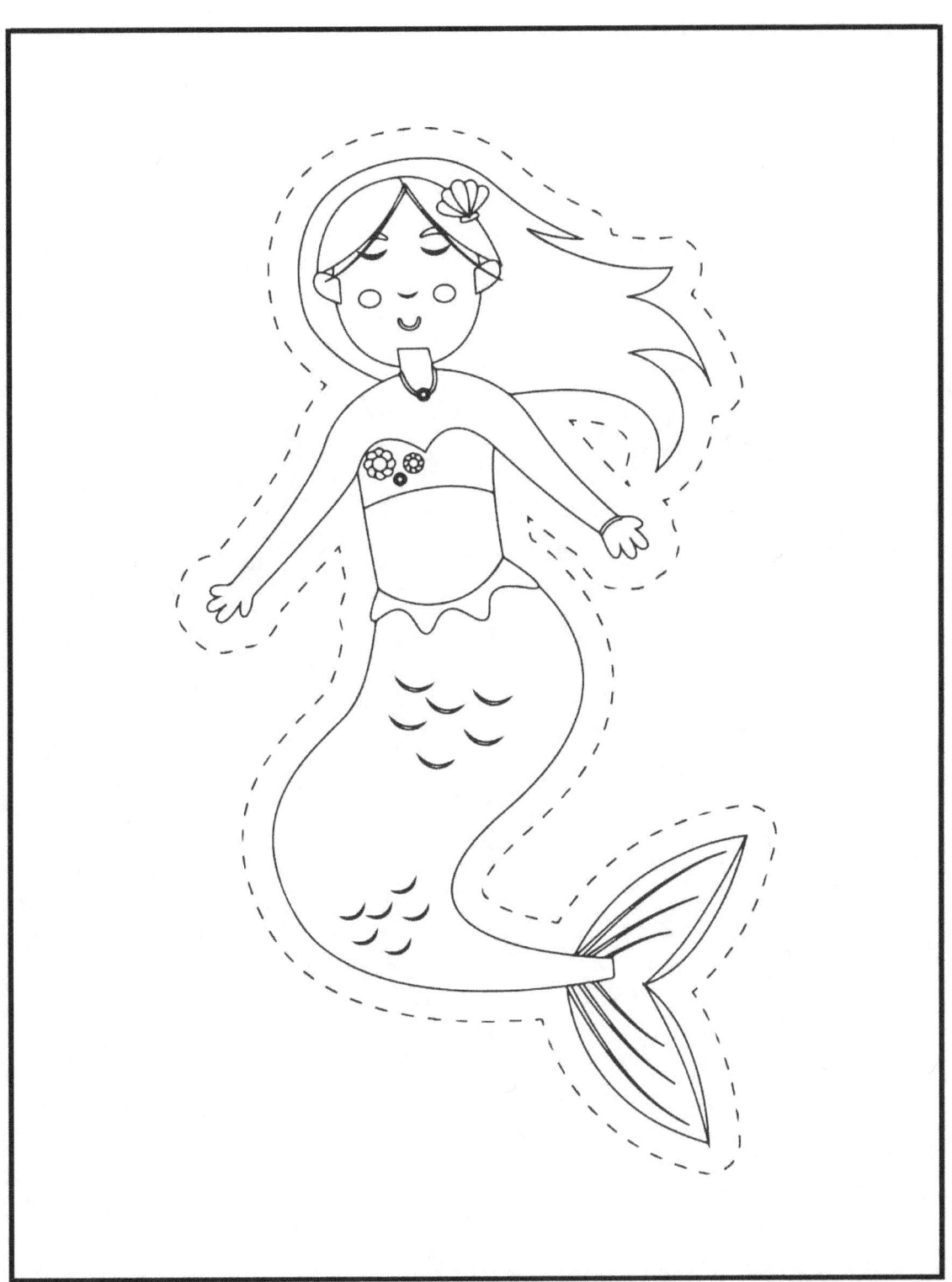

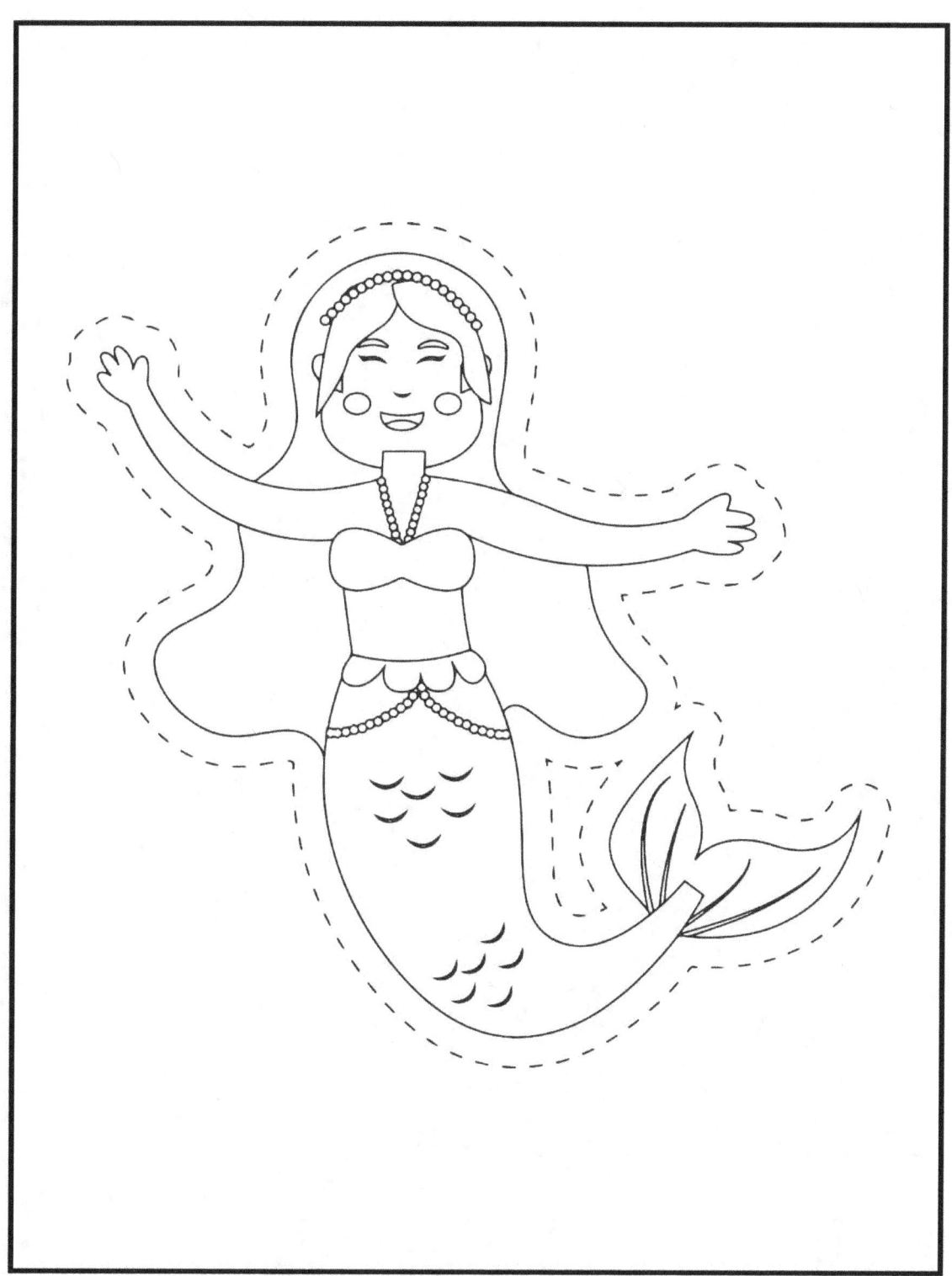

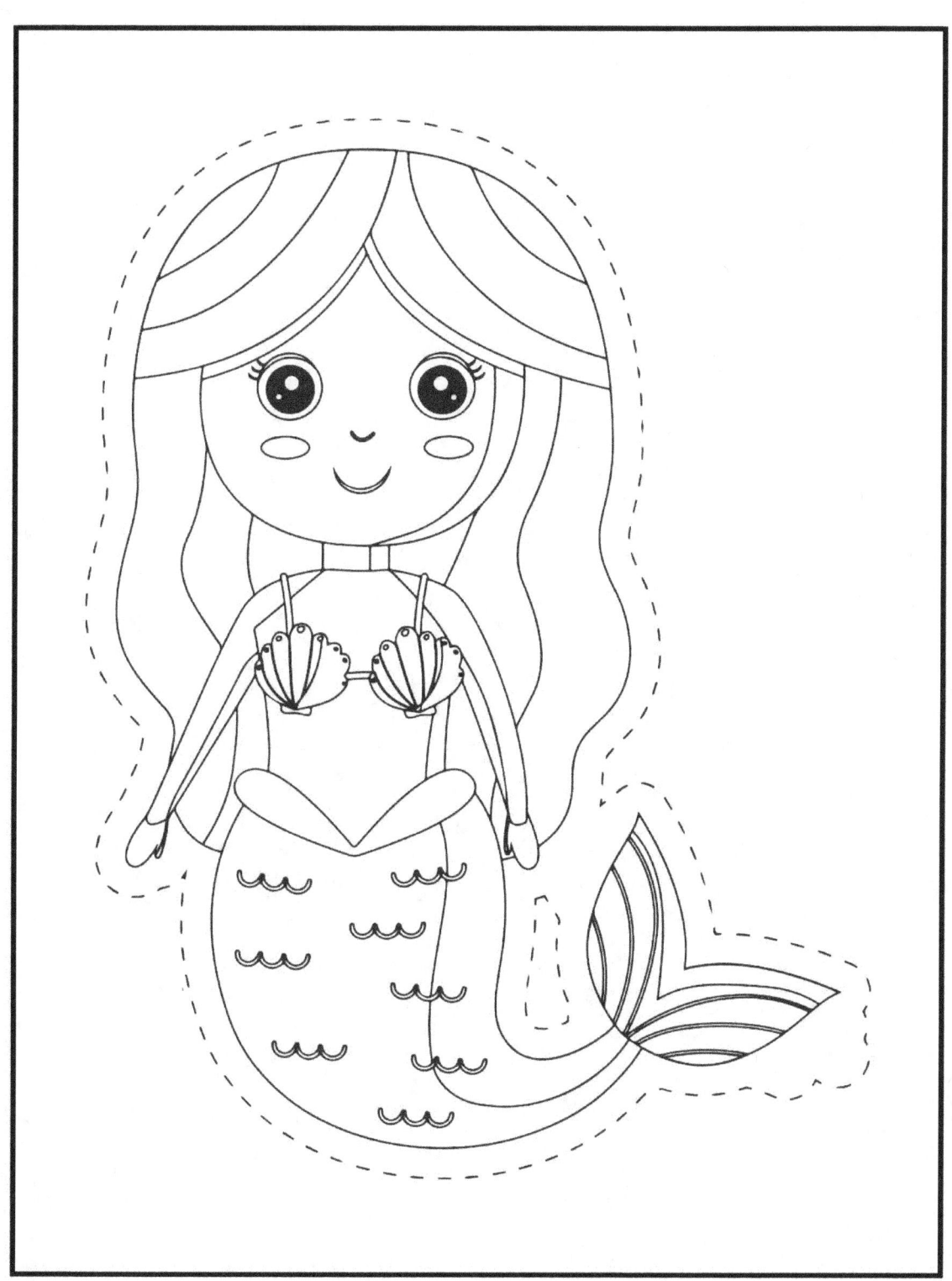

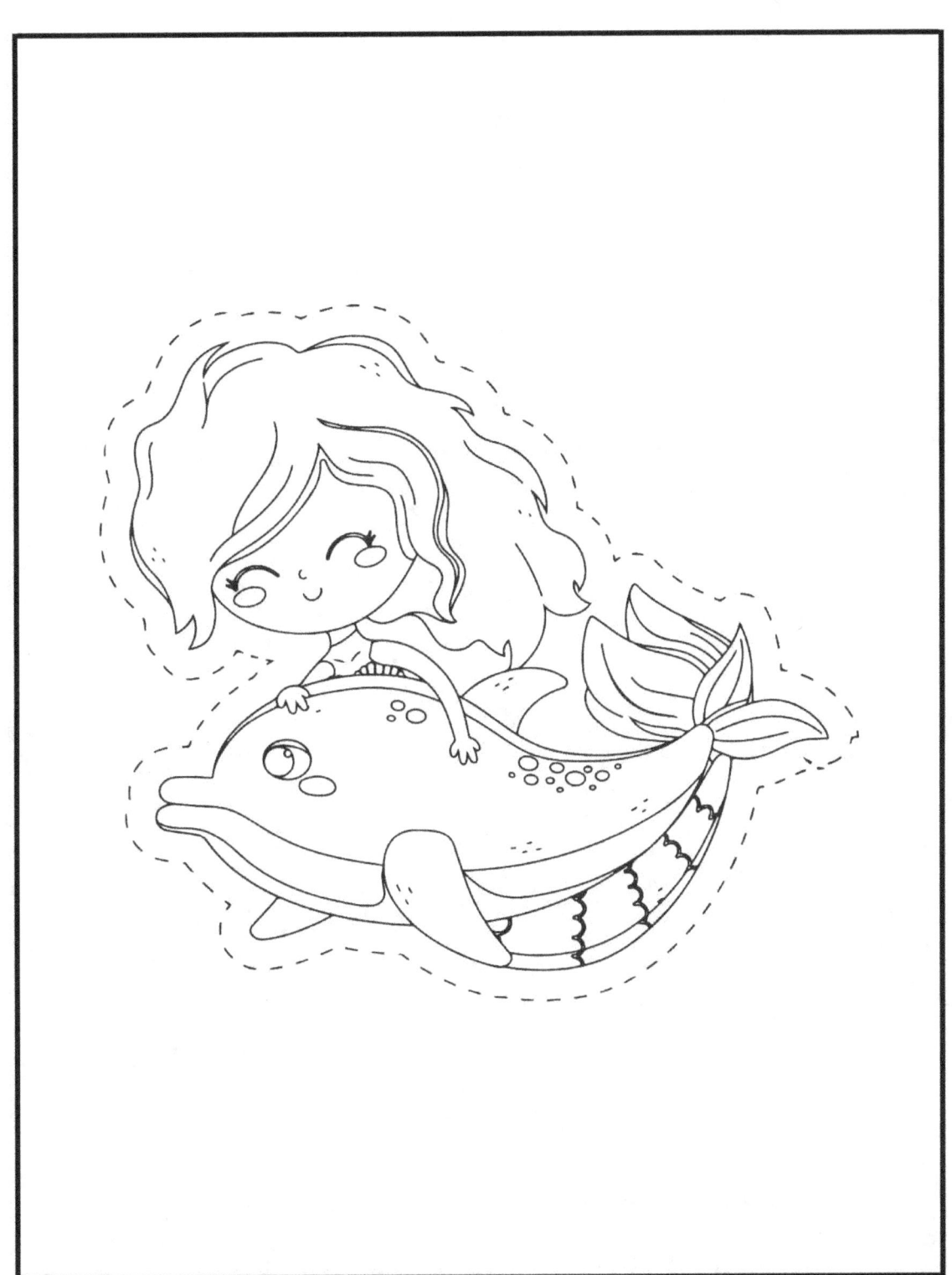

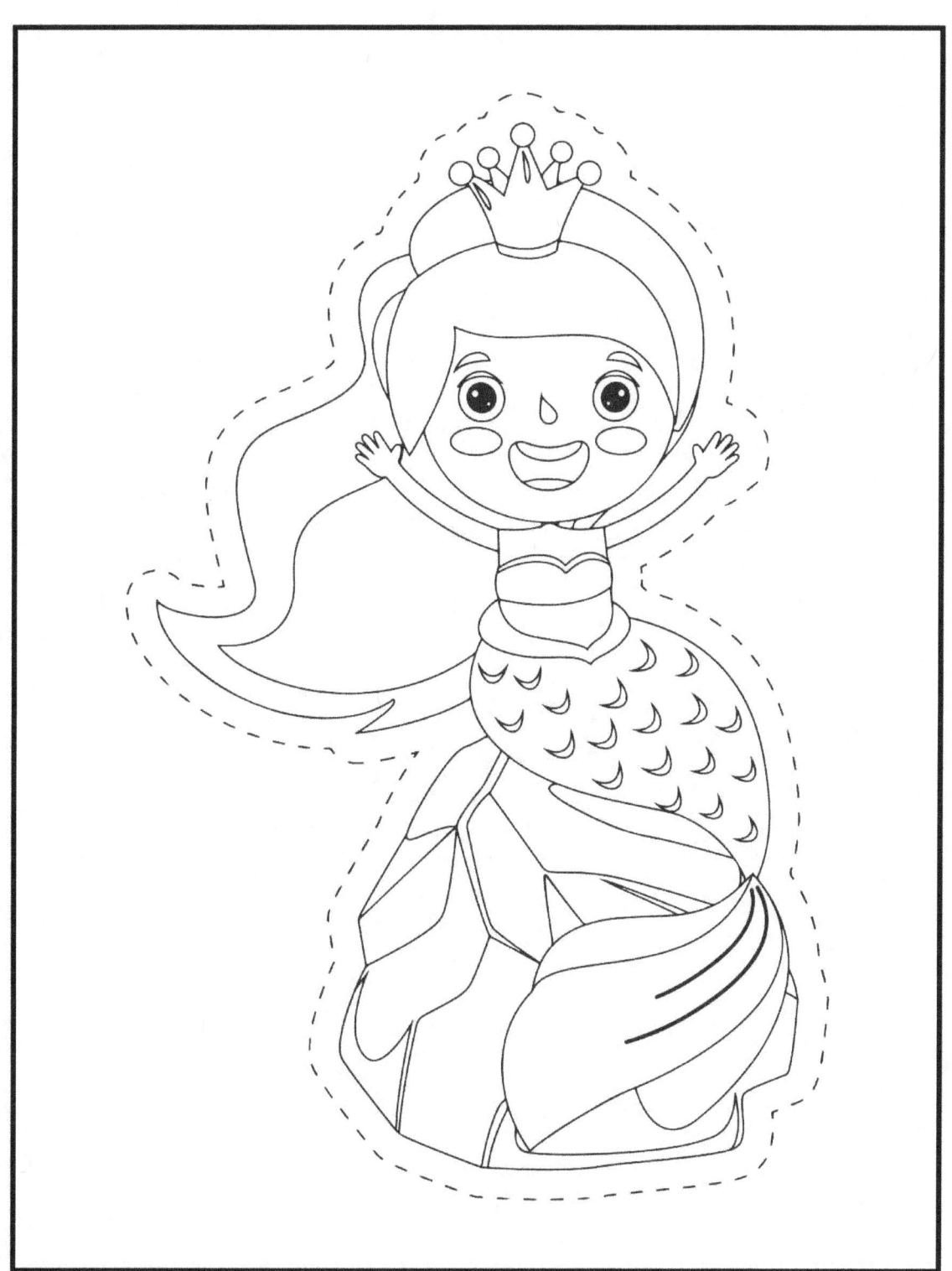

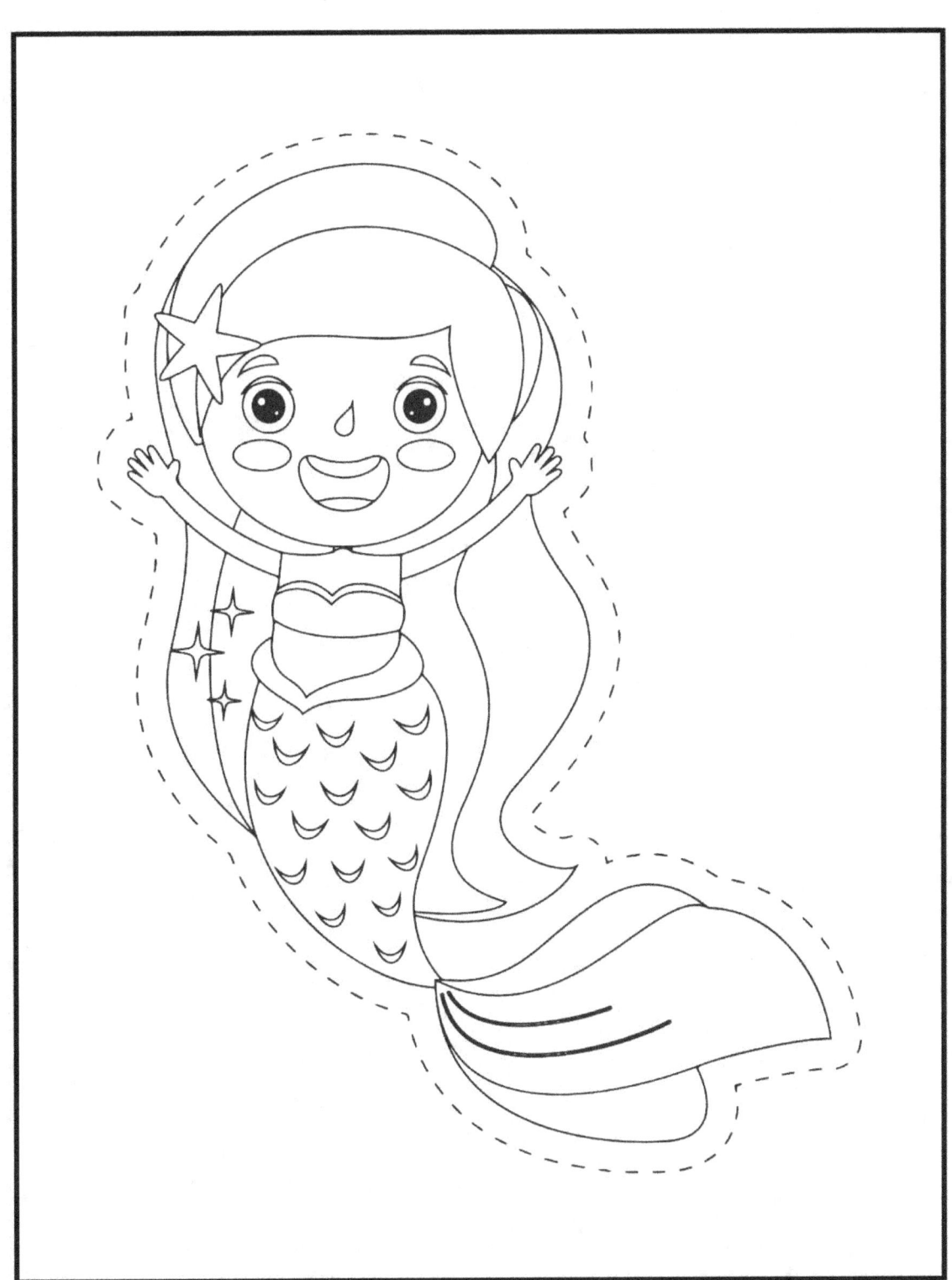

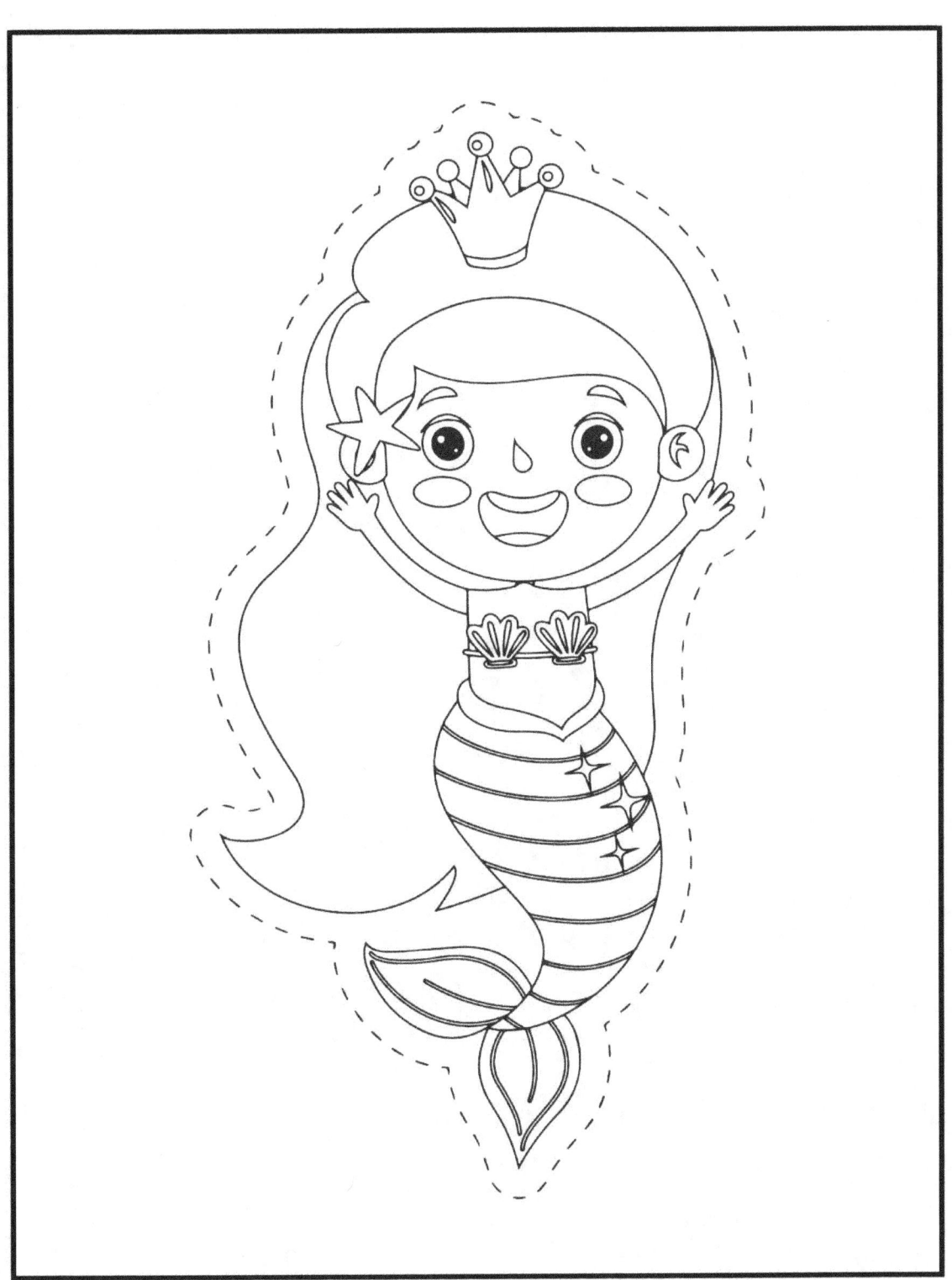

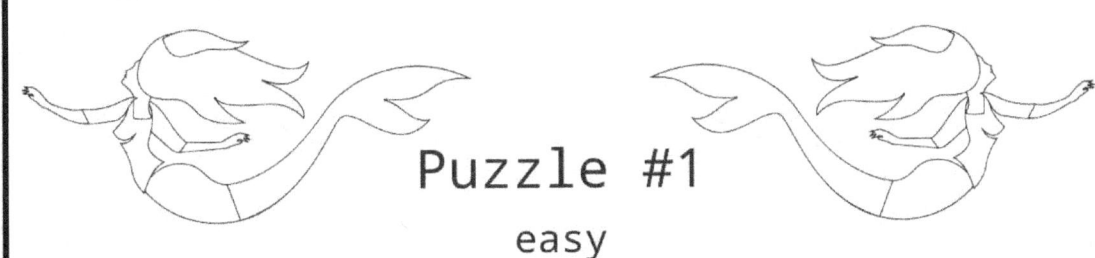

Puzzle #1
easy

	8	2	9		7	6	4	
6	3	7	2		8			
5		4				2		
	1		3		4	9		6
				6			8	
3	4							
			8		2			7
8	2	1	7	9	3	4		
		3	4		5			2

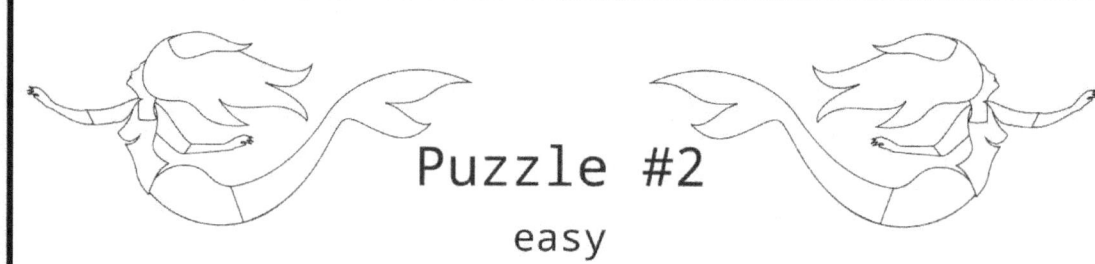

Puzzle #2
easy

1		5		7			9	2
		9			8			4
	7		2	9		1		5
	5	6				4		
2	1	7			6	5	3	9
					5		6	1
9	4		8					
		8		4		2	1	
		1	3	5			4	

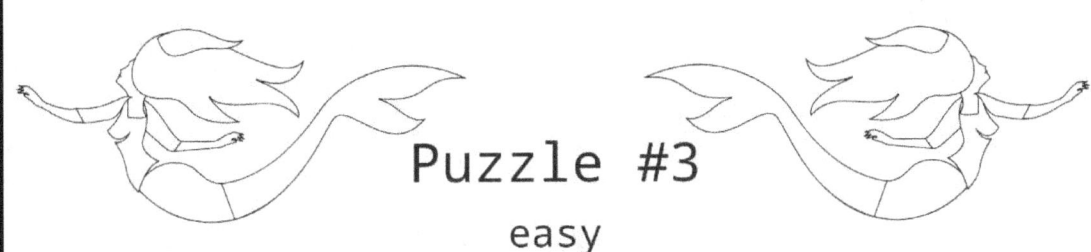

Puzzle #3
easy

	7	4	1	3	5			
		1					5	
8			9					3
6	8	2	7	4				9
1		3	6	5	8		4	
		5			9	8		
3		9		4		1		
	6	8	2					4
		7				2	8	6

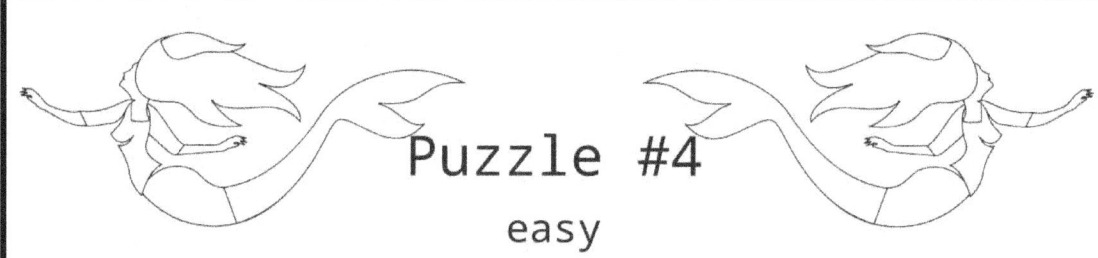

Puzzle #4
easy

			1	5		7	9	8
9		7		2			1	
5			3	7			2	
					5		4	1
8	4	1		3	7			
			6	4				7
6			7			5	8	
				6		4		
3	7	4			2		6	

Puzzle #5
easy

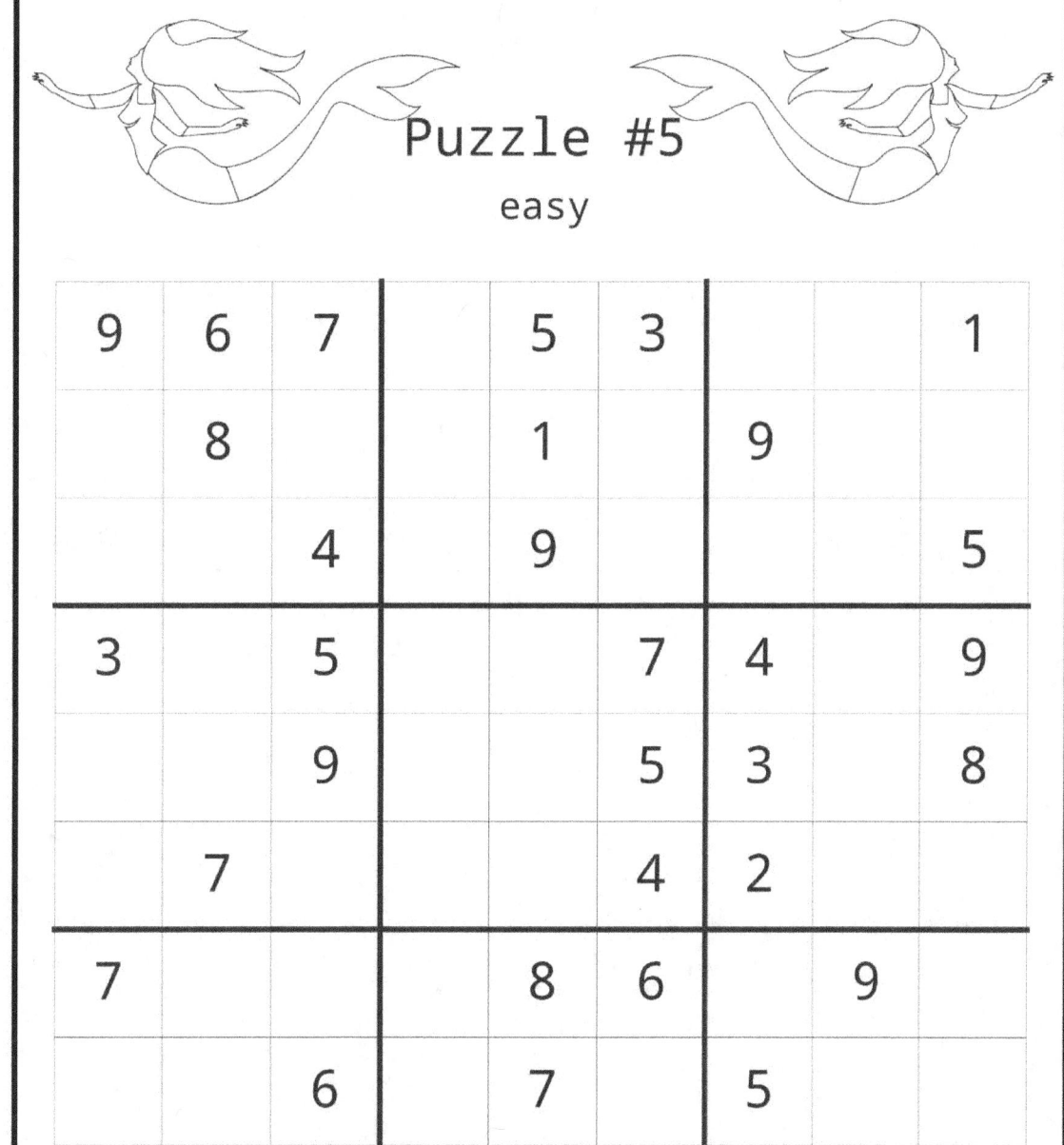

9	6	7		5	3			1
	8			1		9		
		4		9				5
3		5			7	4		9
		9			5	3		8
	7				4	2		
7				8	6		9	
		6		7		5		
1	3	8	5				6	

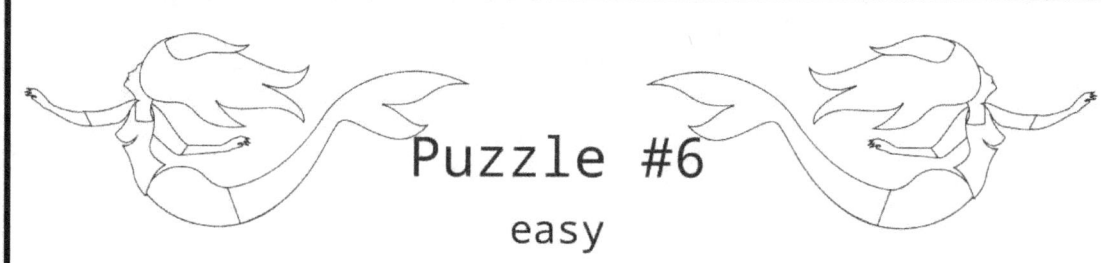

Puzzle #6
easy

5		8					4		9
3	4	9			5	1	6	2
			9	4			7	8
		3			6			1
			1	9		6		
6			5		8	2		7
	6	4			2			
	3	7	8					6
8	1						2	

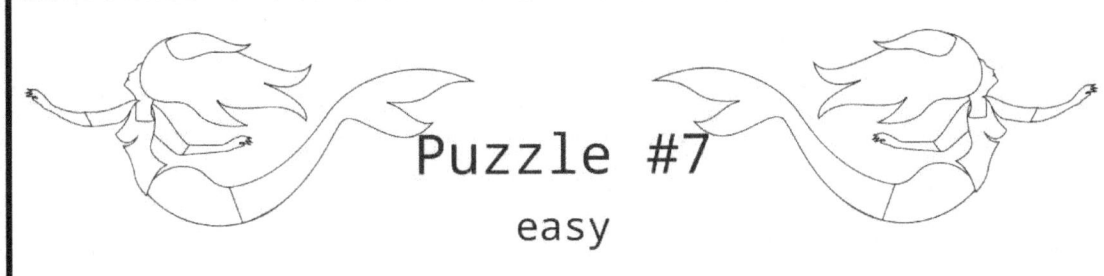

Puzzle #7
easy

	4				1	3	7	9
	1	5				8	6	
			8		6	4		
	6	3	2			5		1
5	2			3				
	8	7	9				2	
6	9	2	7	4	5		3	
							9	6
			6	8		2		

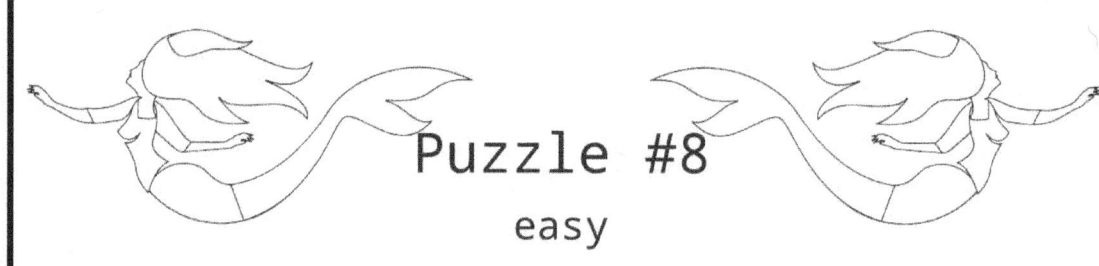

Puzzle #8
easy

		2	6	5		1		
8				2		4	7	
	5				4	8		2
3	7		4	8		9		
					5		4	8
6	8	4						
	1			4			8	
					2	6	9	
9	2	6		7	3		1	

The Dot Game

Take turns connecting the dots until you make a square. Put your initials in each square. At the end, the person with the most squares win.

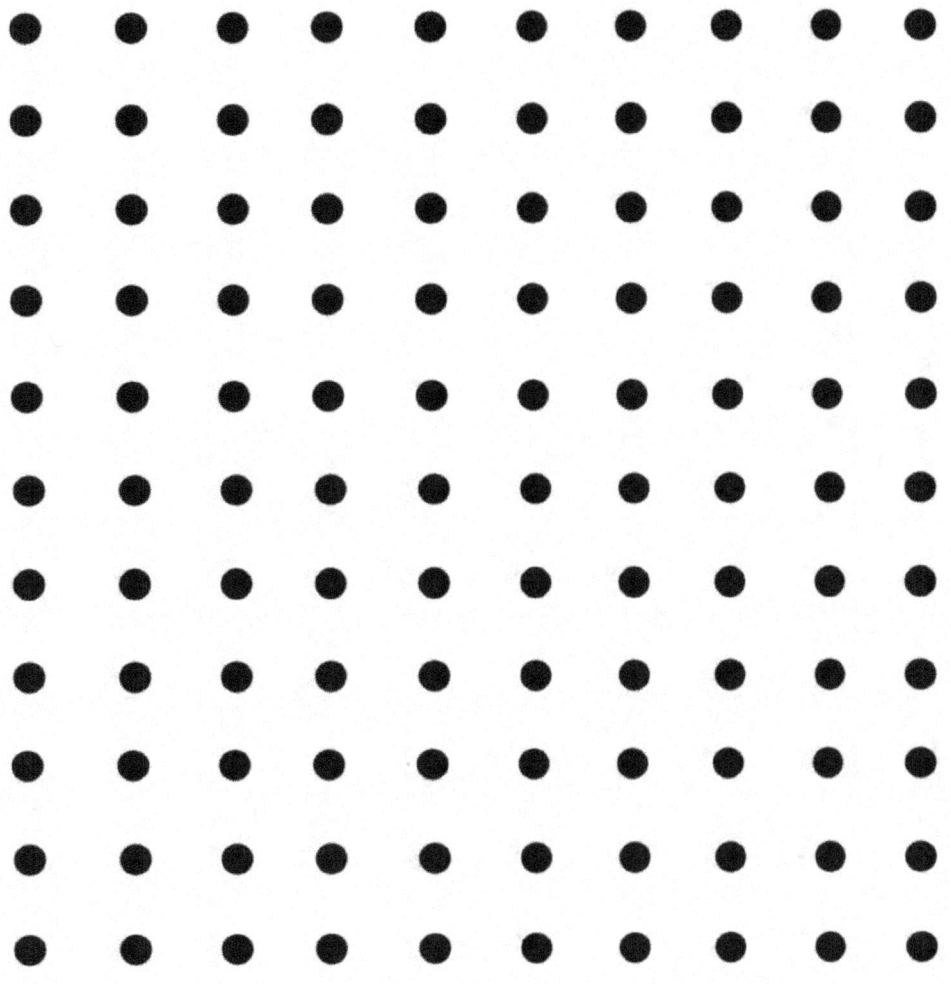

The Dot Game

Take turns connecting the dots until you make a square. Put your initials in each square. At the end, the person with the most squares win.

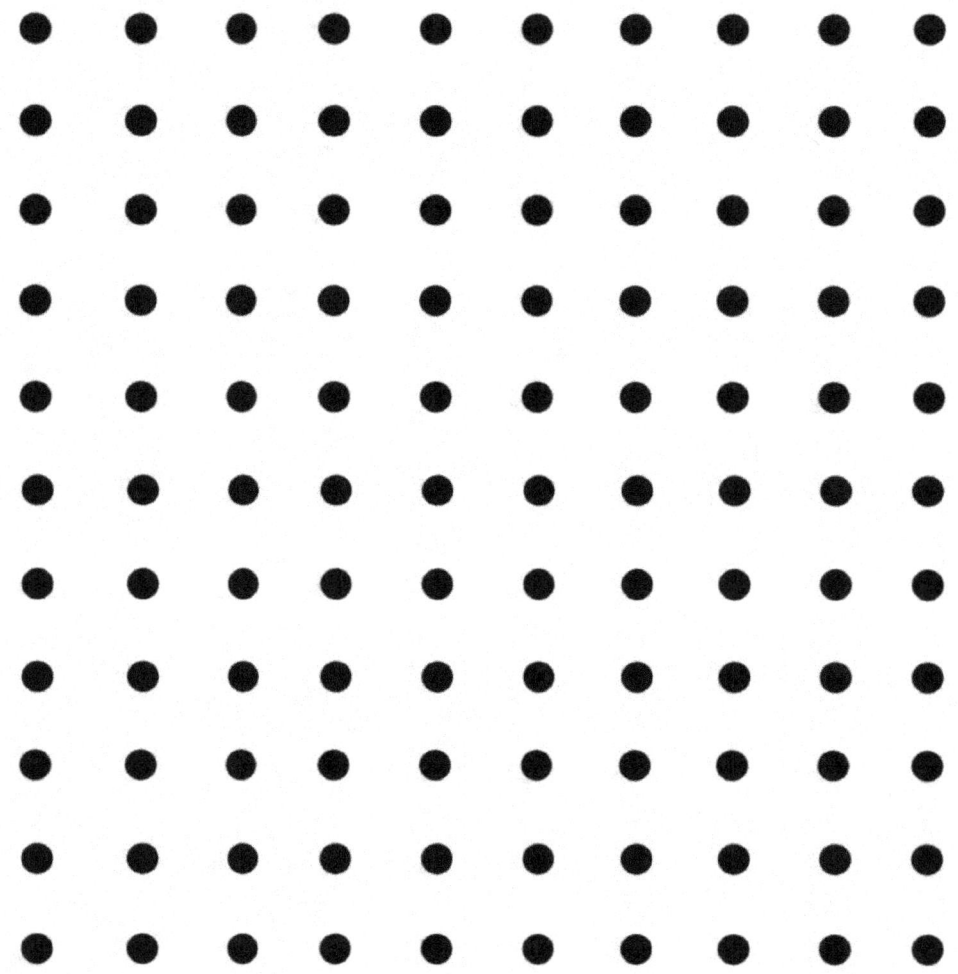

The Dot Game

Take turns connecting the dots until you make a square. Put your initials in each square. At the end, the person with the most squares win.

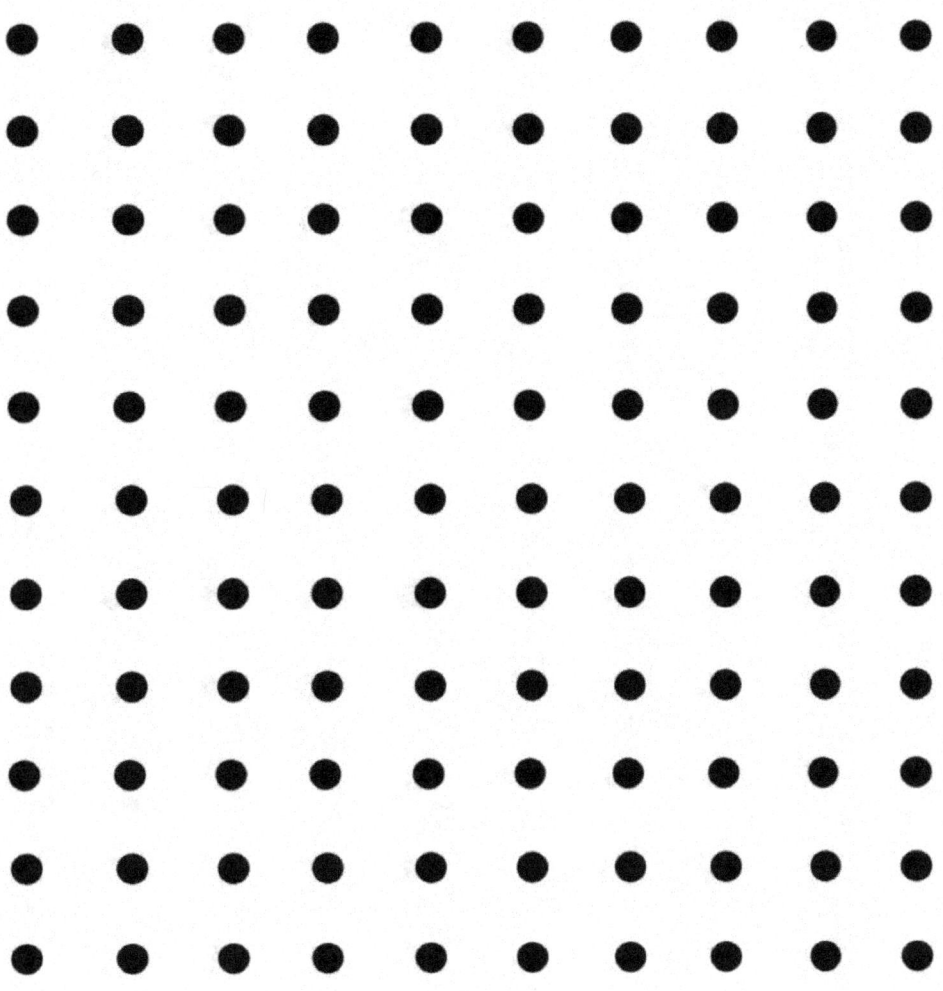

The Dot Game

Take turns connecting the dots until you make a square. Put your initials in each square. At the end, the person with the most squares win.

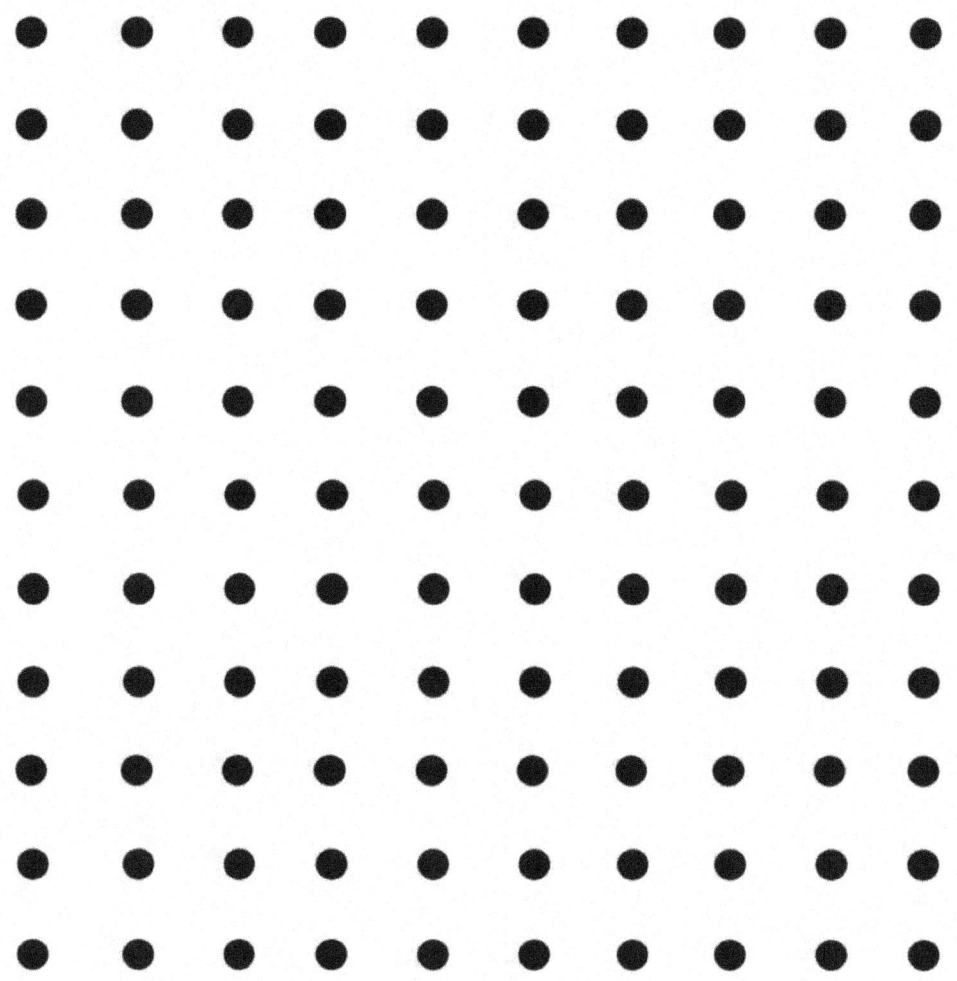

The Dot Game

Take turns connecting the dots until you make a square. Put your initials in each square. At the end, the person with the most squares win.

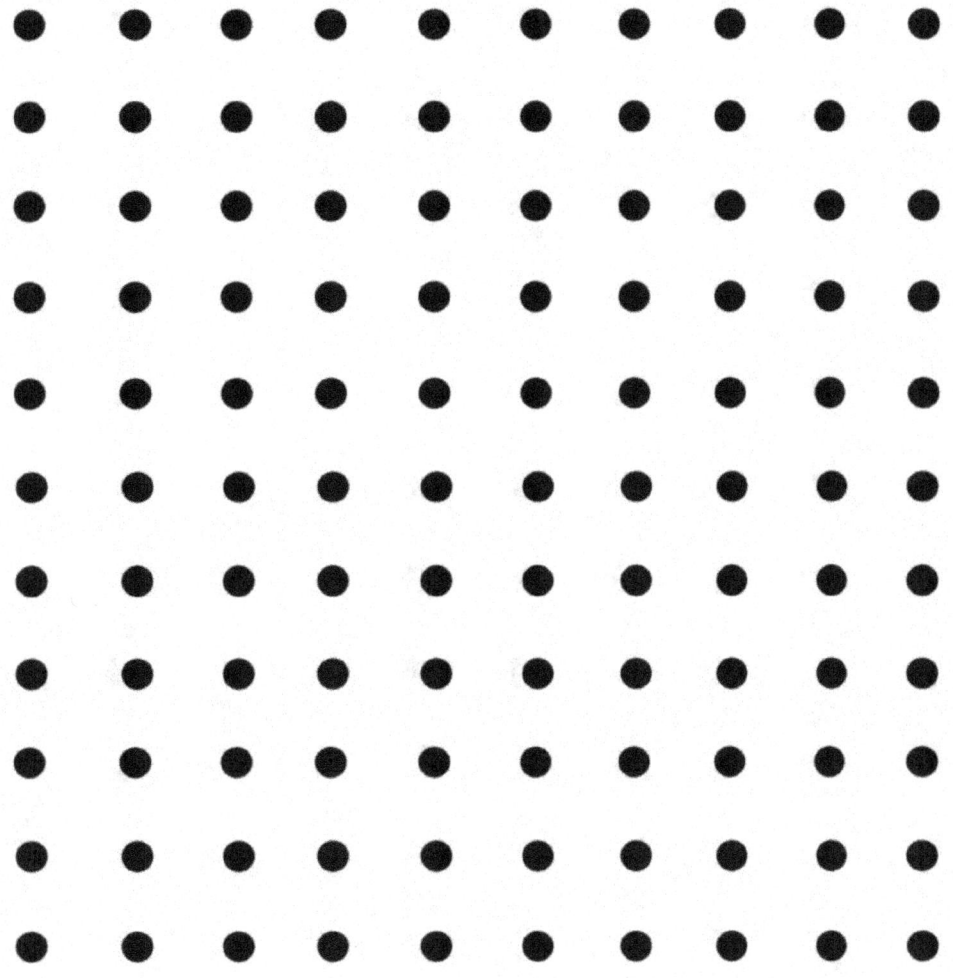

The Dot Game

Take turns connecting the dots until you make a square. Put your initials in each square. At the end, the person with the most squares win.

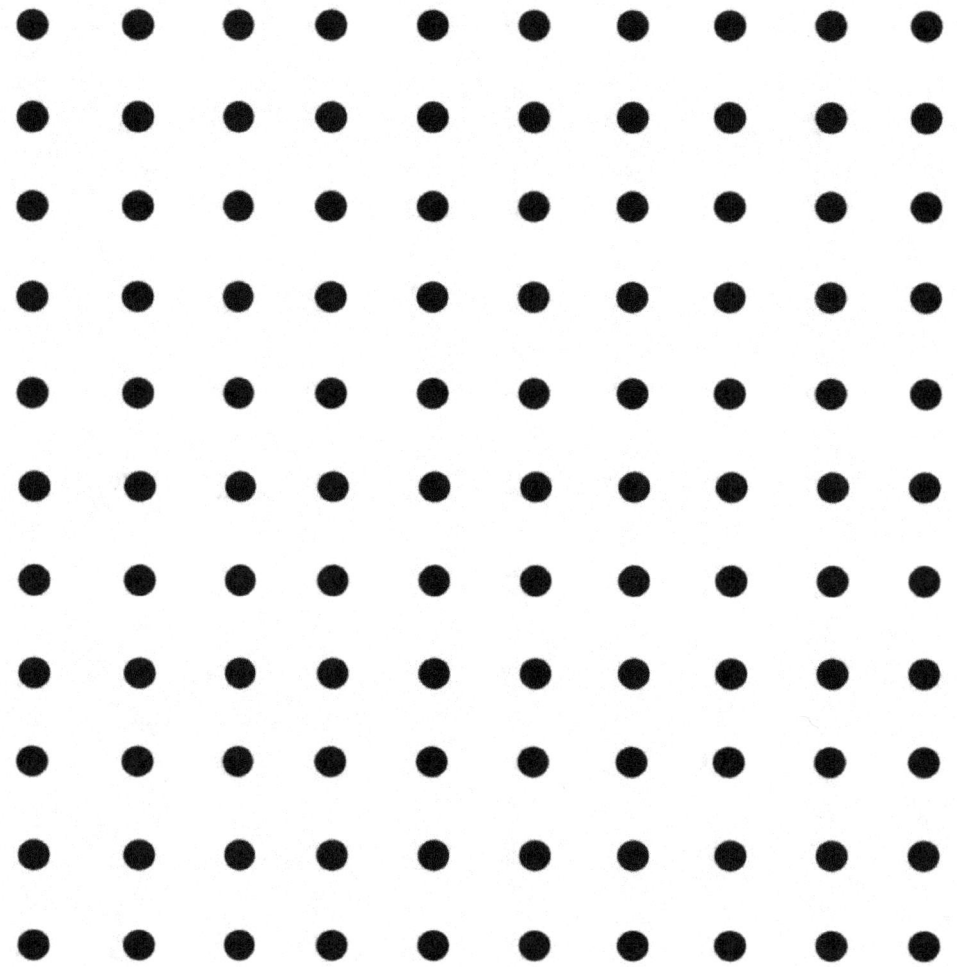

The Dot Game

Take turns connecting the dots until you make a square. Put your initials in each square. At the end, the person with the most squares win.

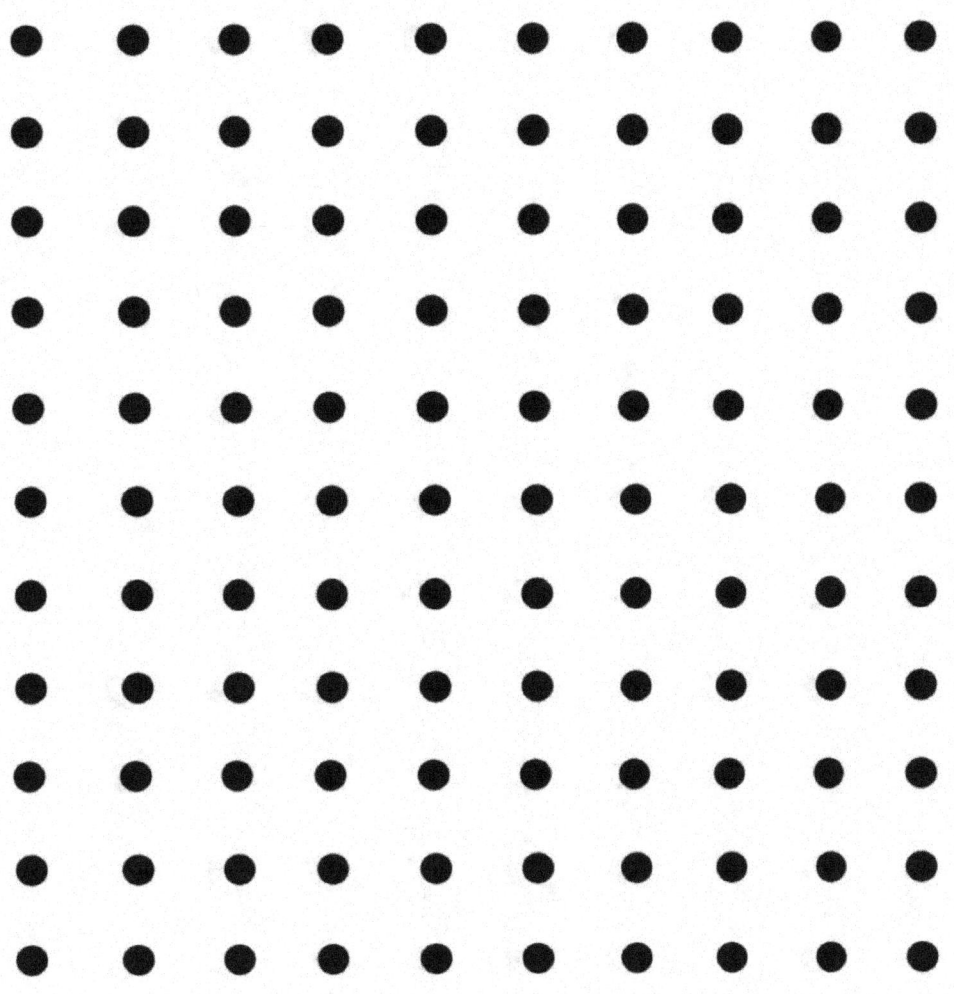

The Dot Game

Take turns connecting the dots until you make a square. Put your initials in each square. At the end, the person with the most squares win.

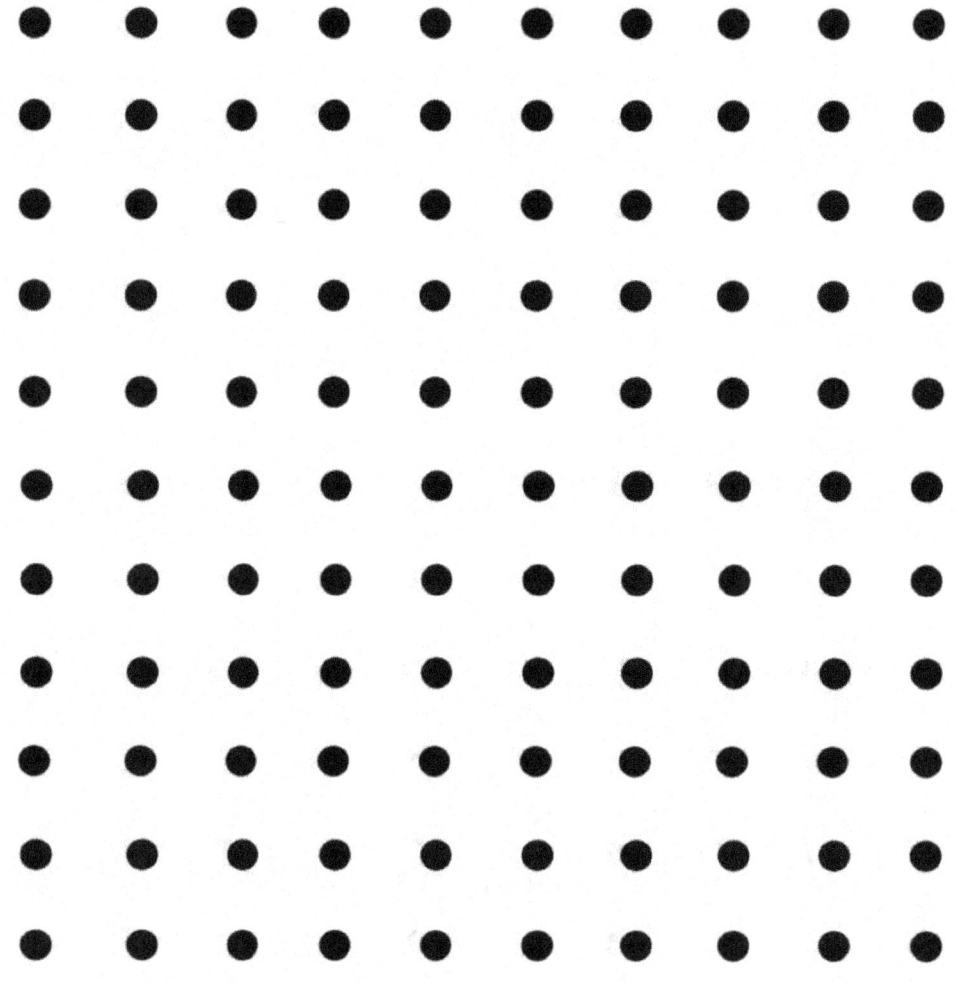

The Dot Game

Take turns connecting the dots until you make a square. Put your initials in each square. At the end, the person with the most squares win.

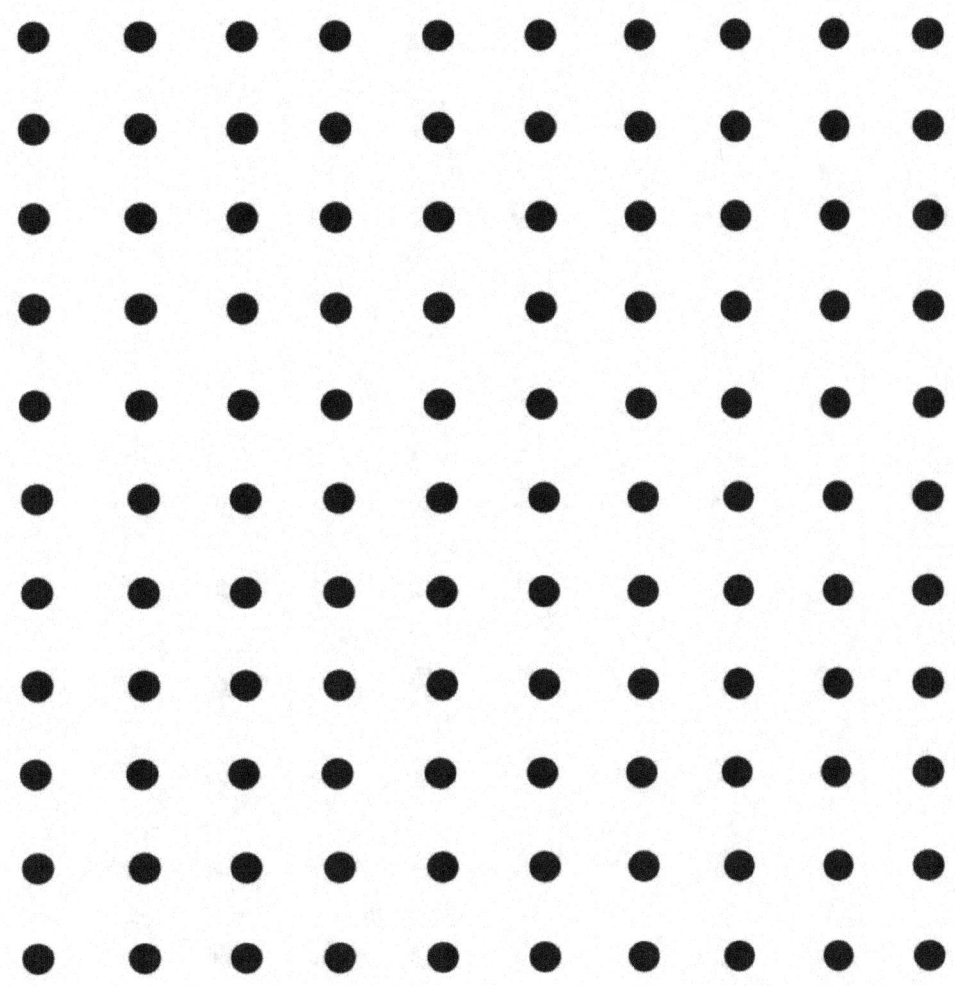

The Dot Game

Take turns connecting the dots until you make a square. Put your initials in each square. At the end, the person with the most squares win.

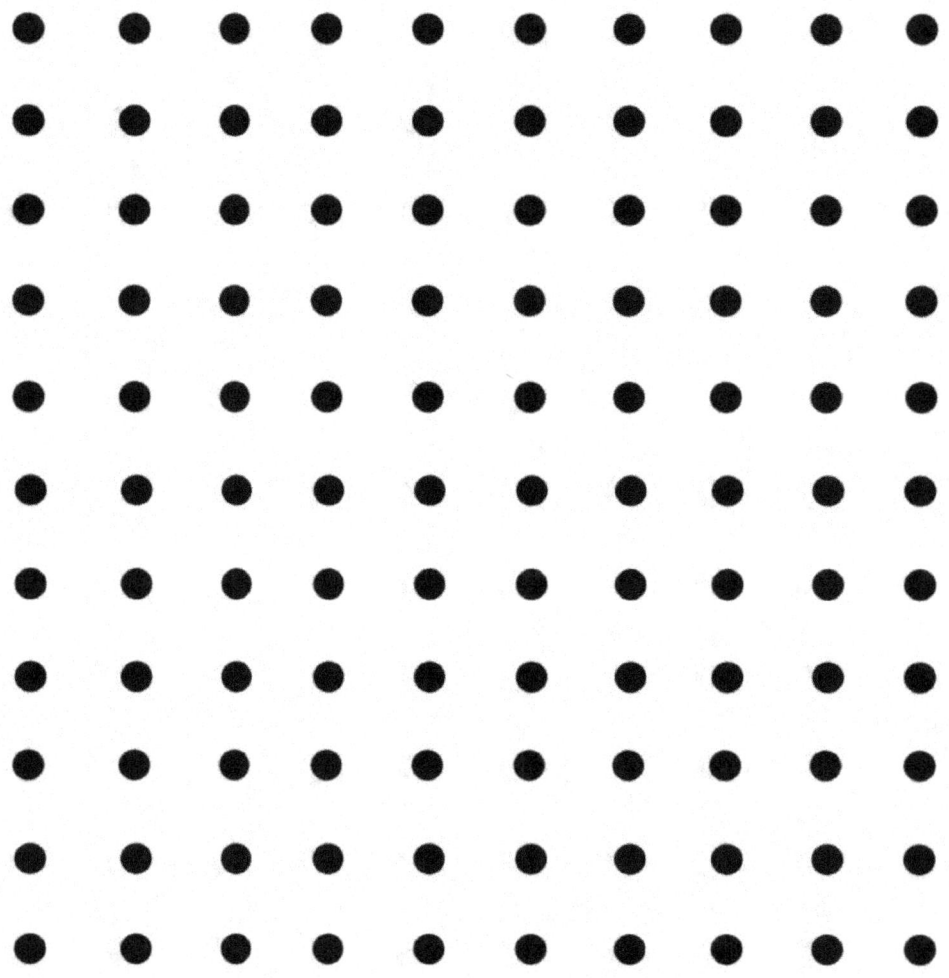

Maze #1

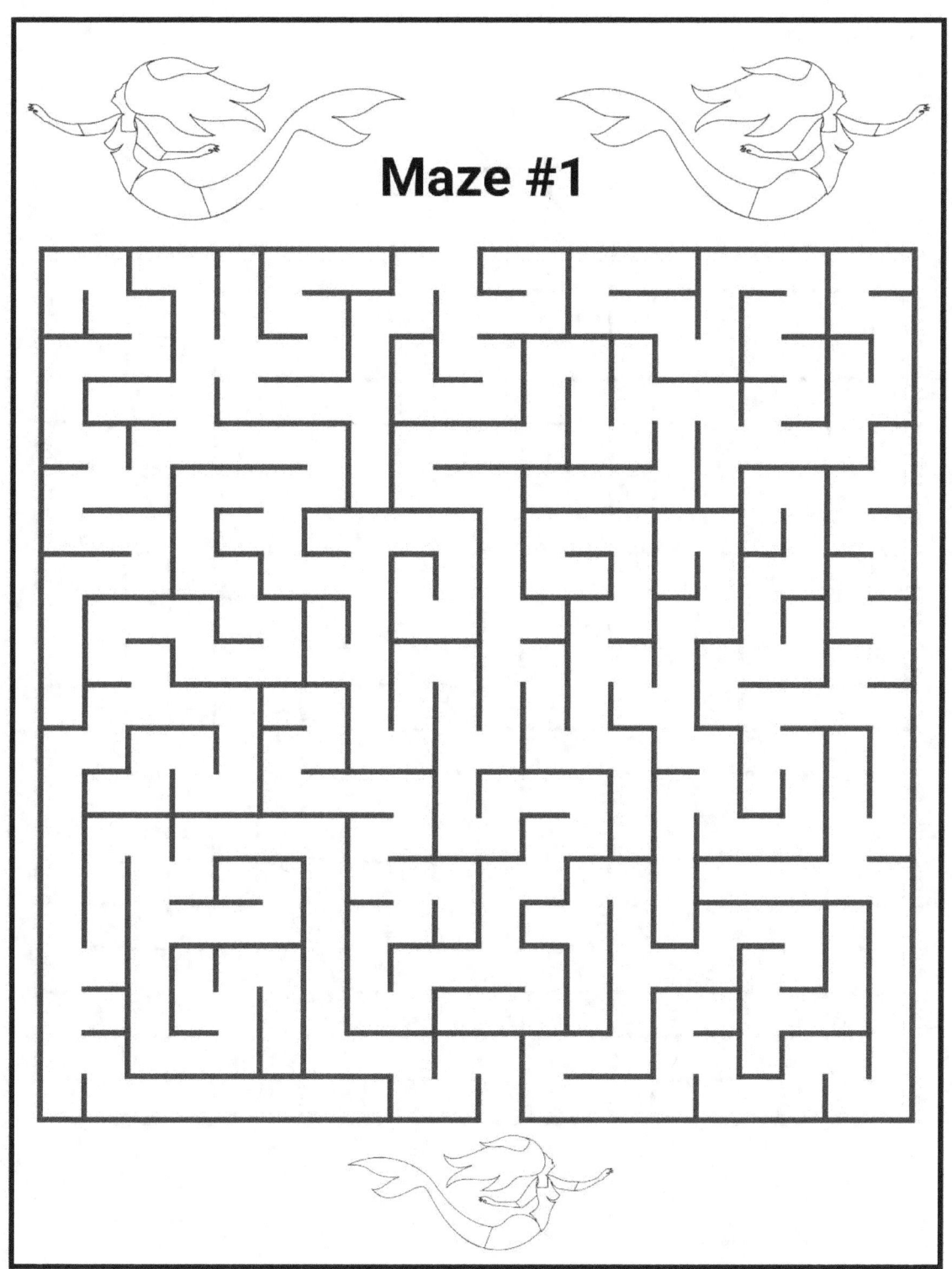

Maze #2

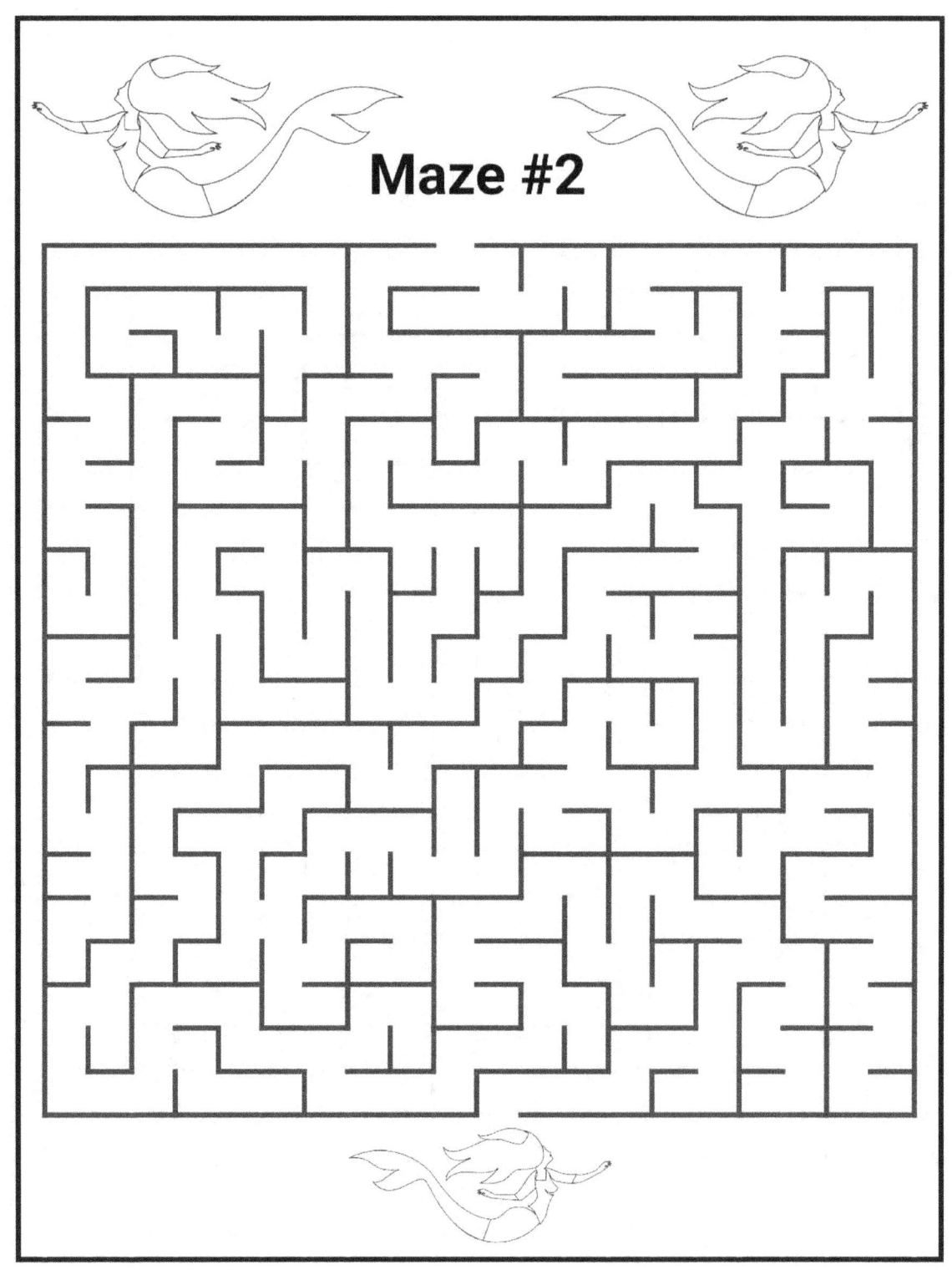

Maze #3

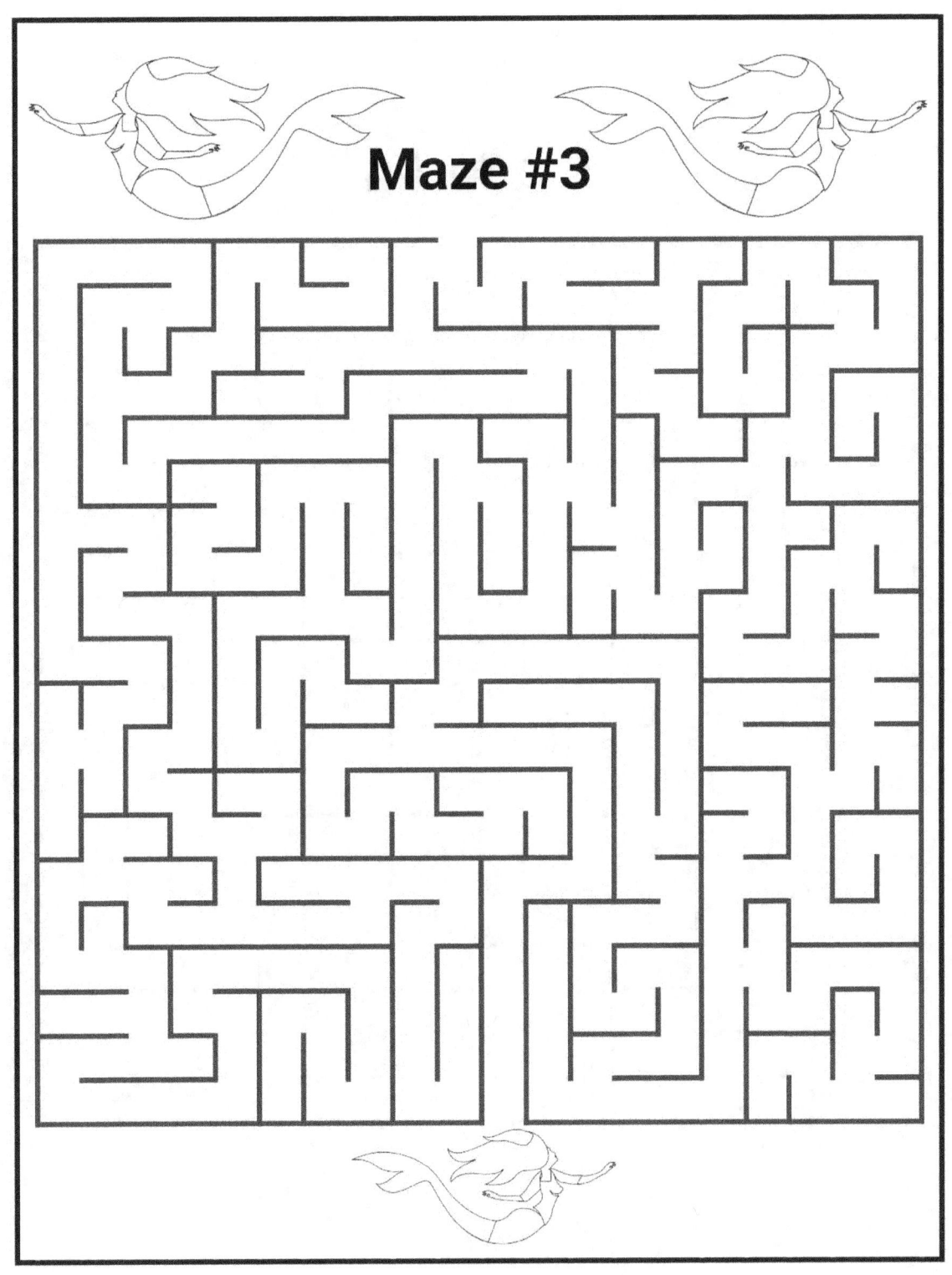

Maze #4

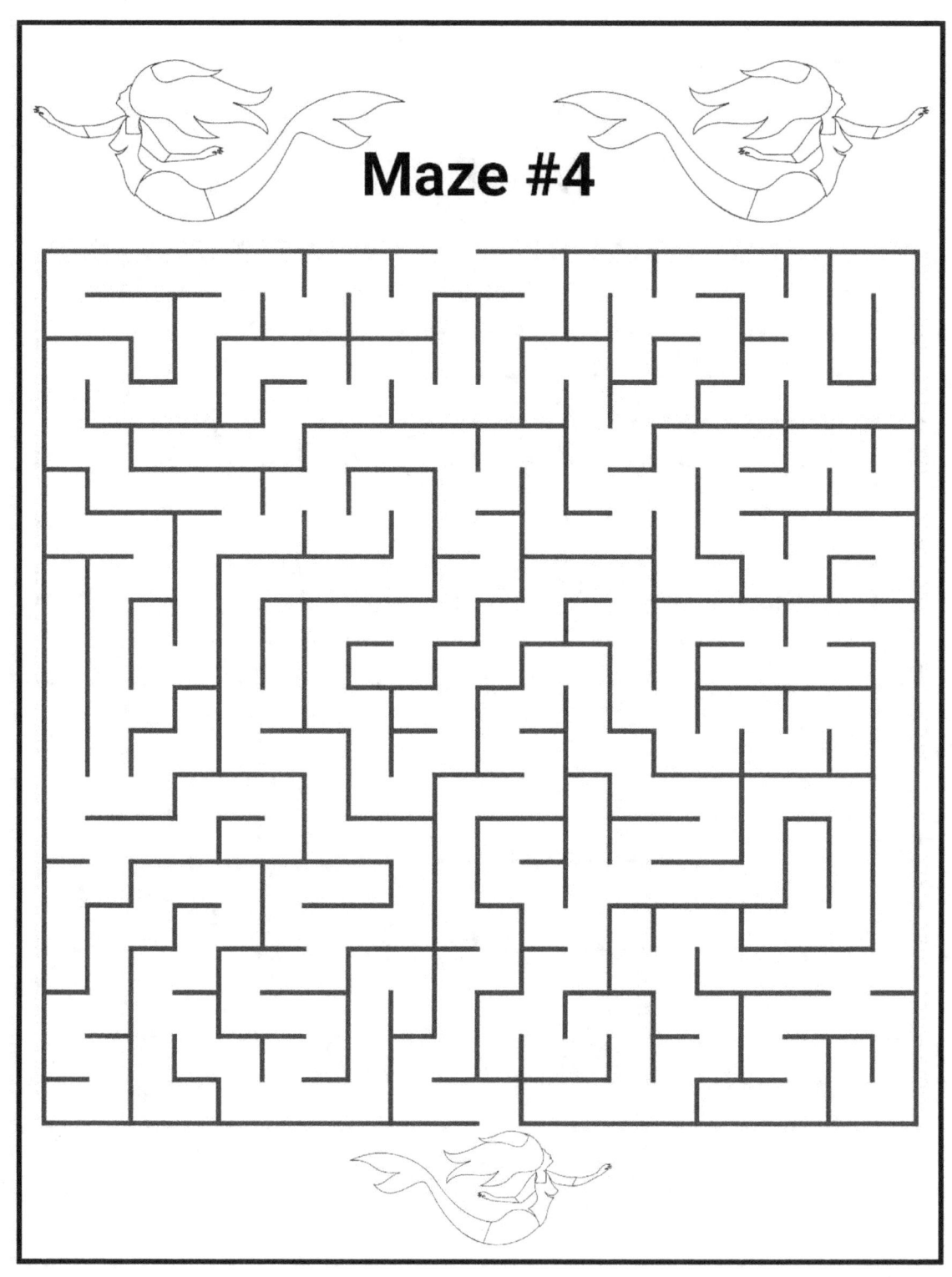

Maze #5

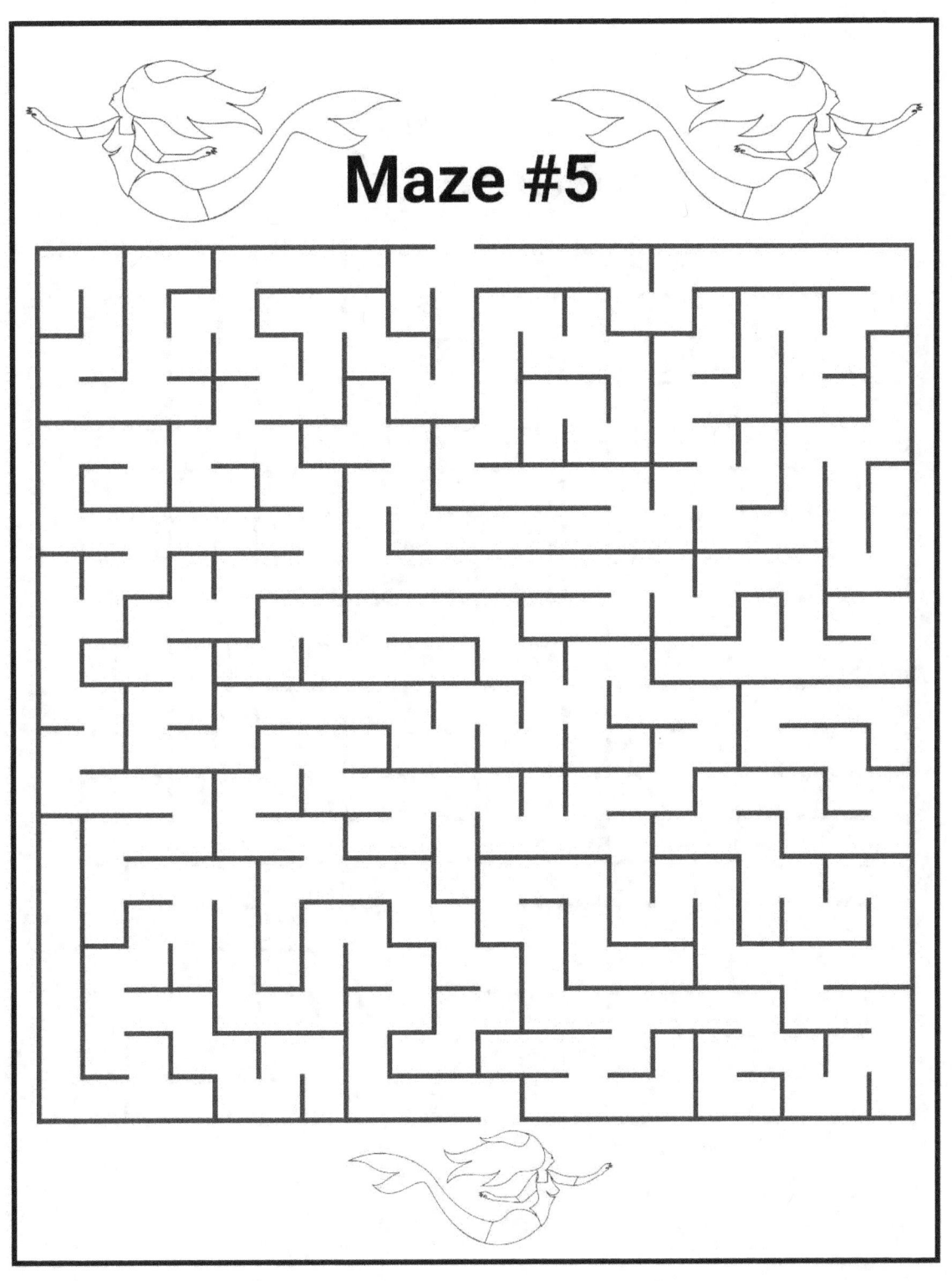

Maze #6

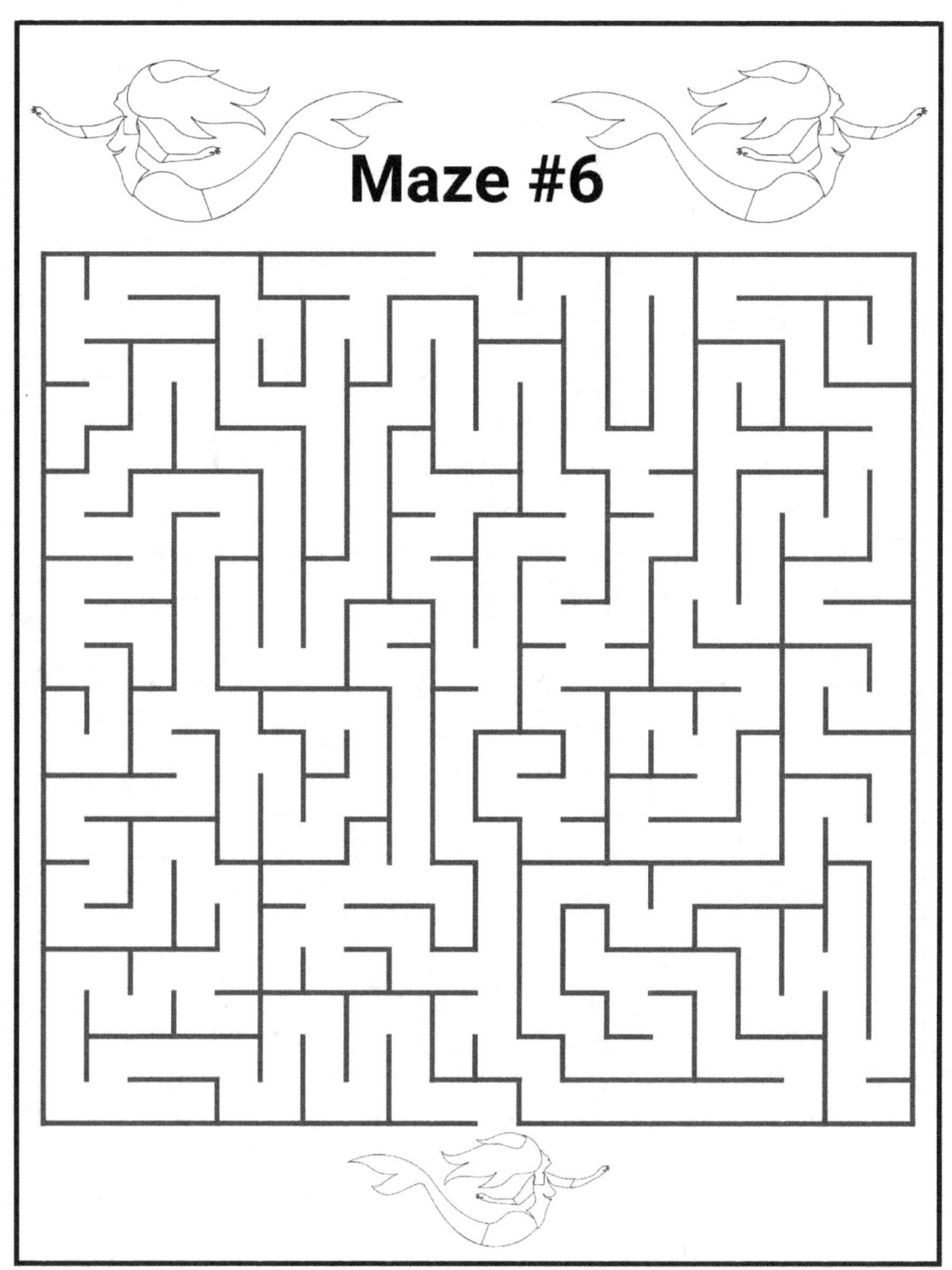

Maze #7

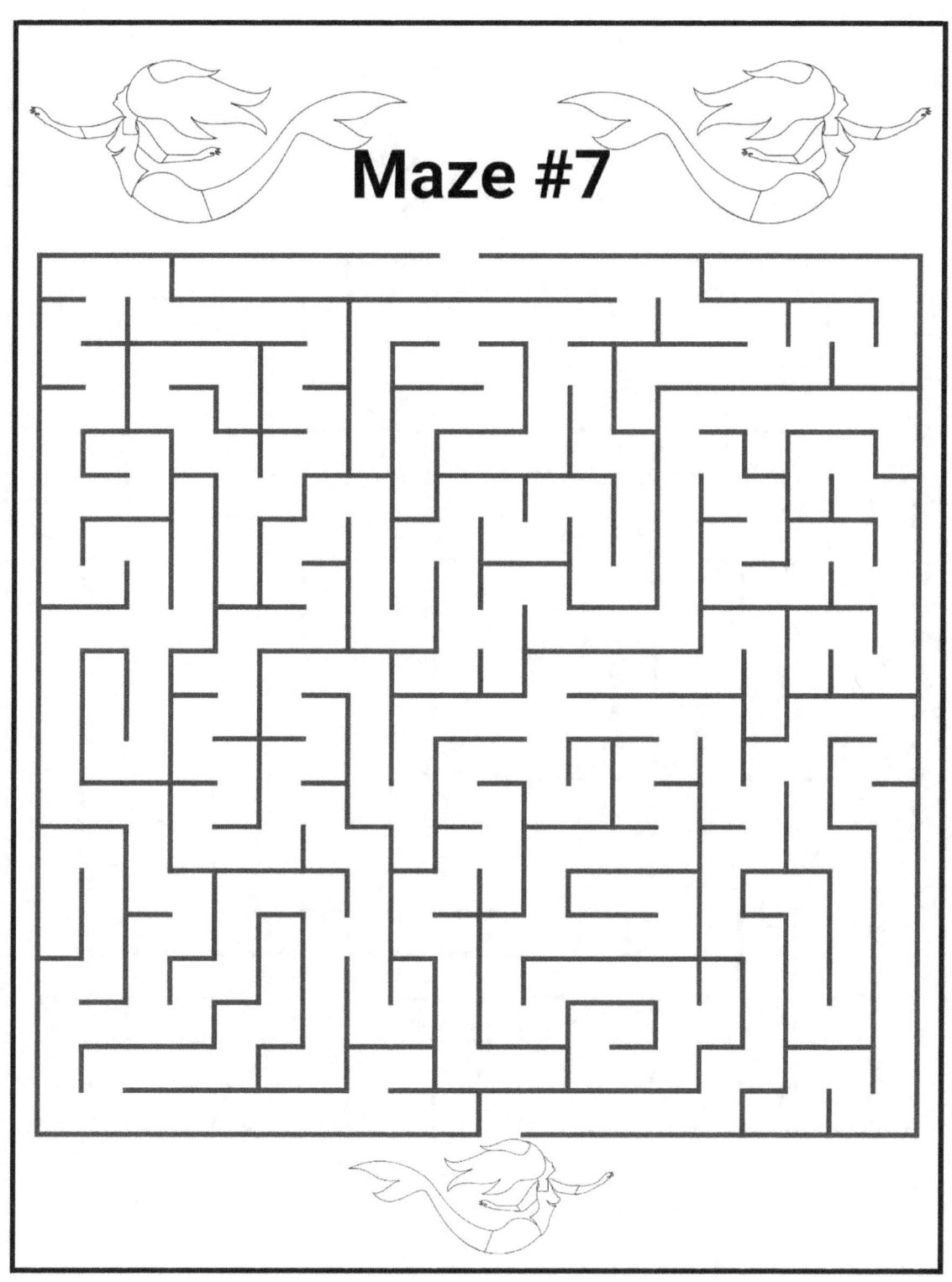

Maze #8

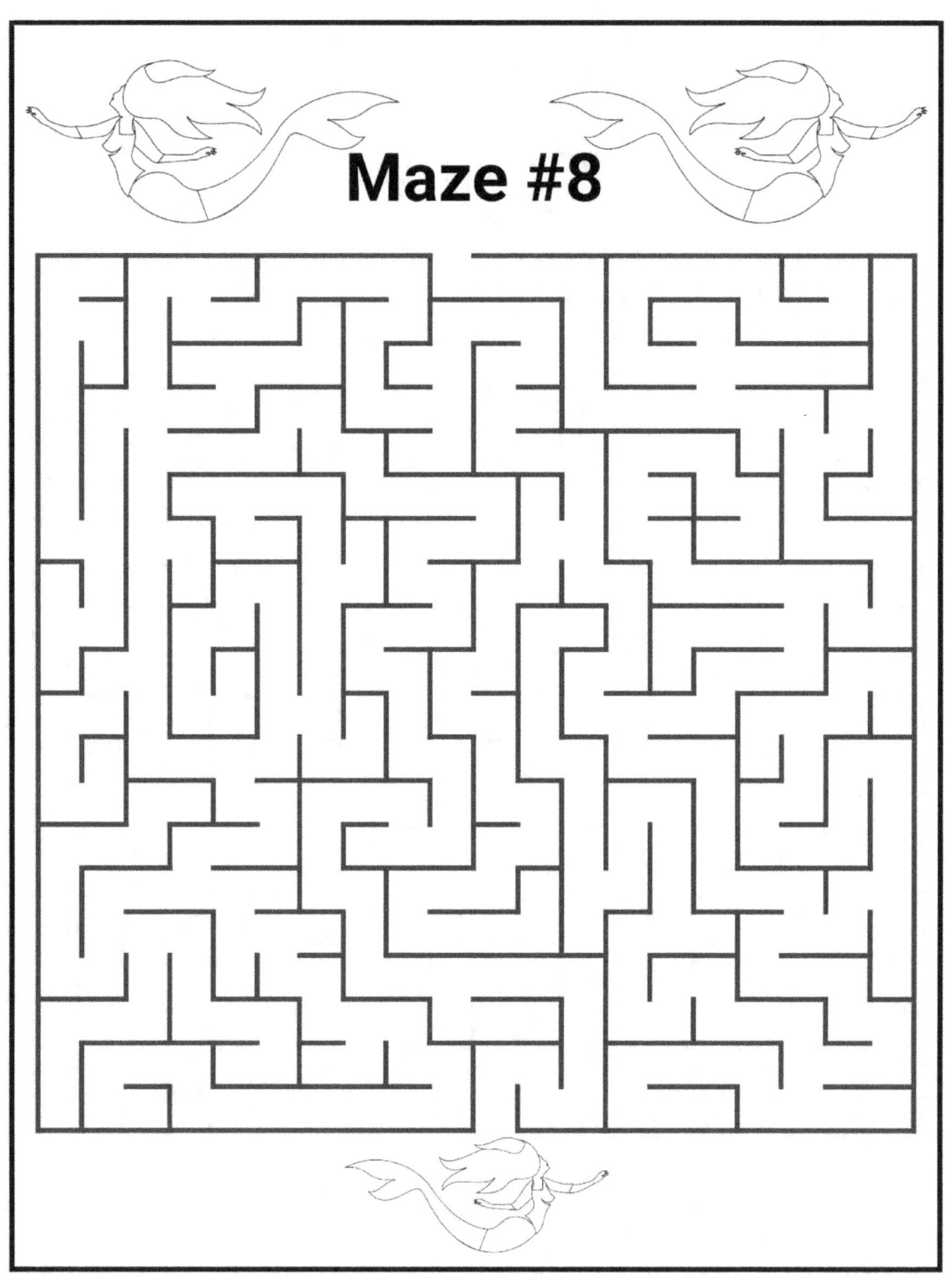

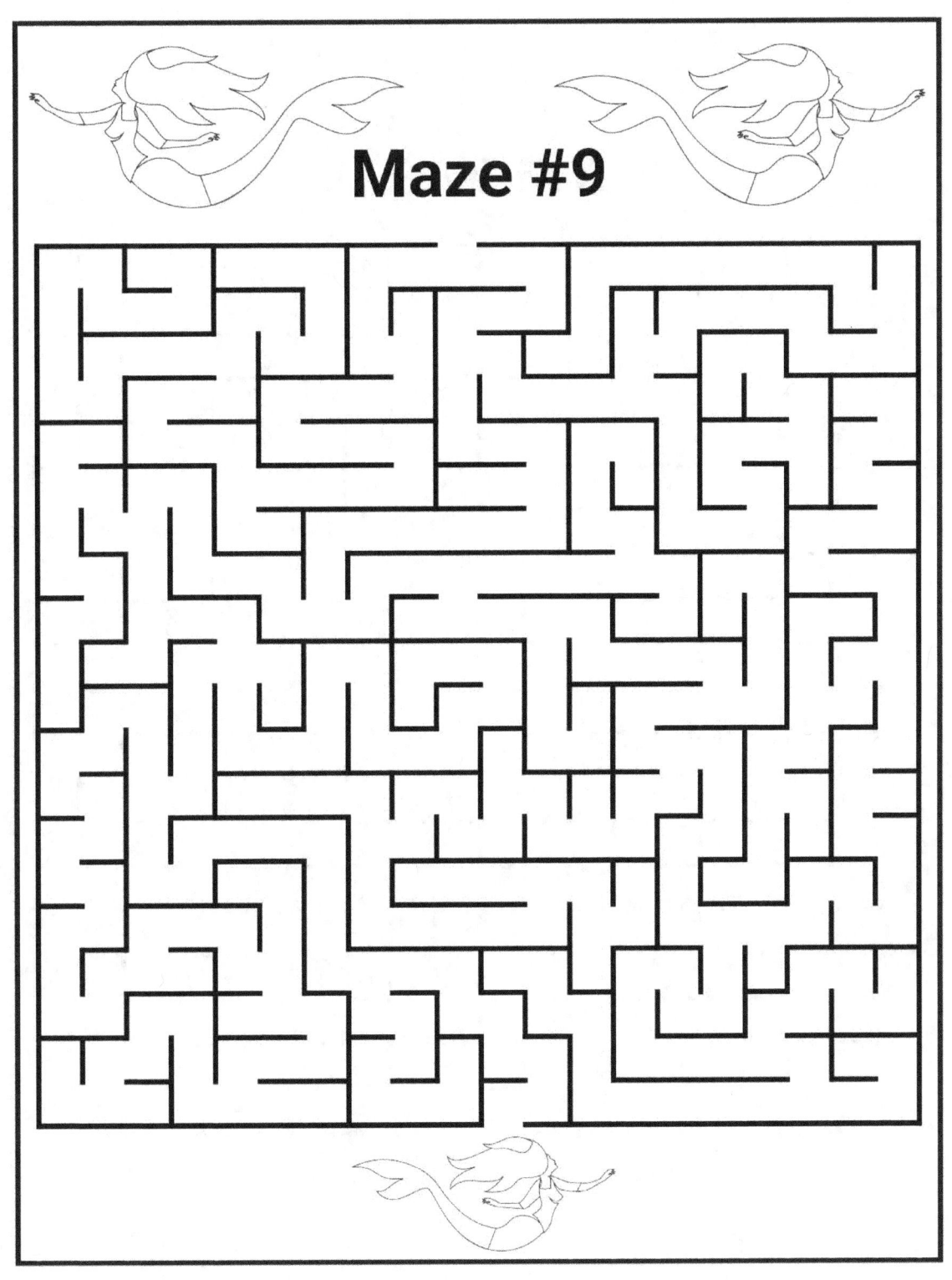

Maze #10

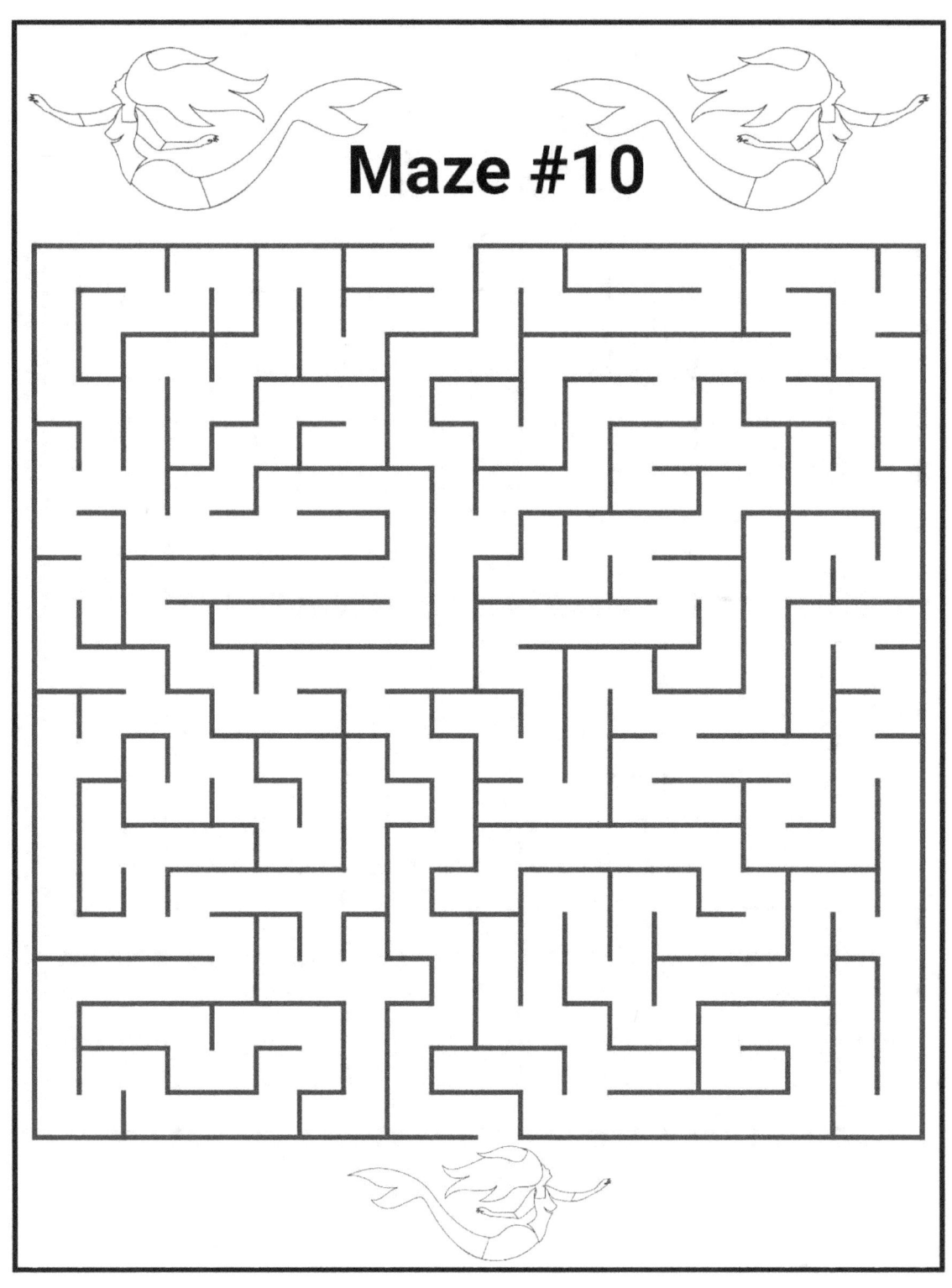

Maze #11

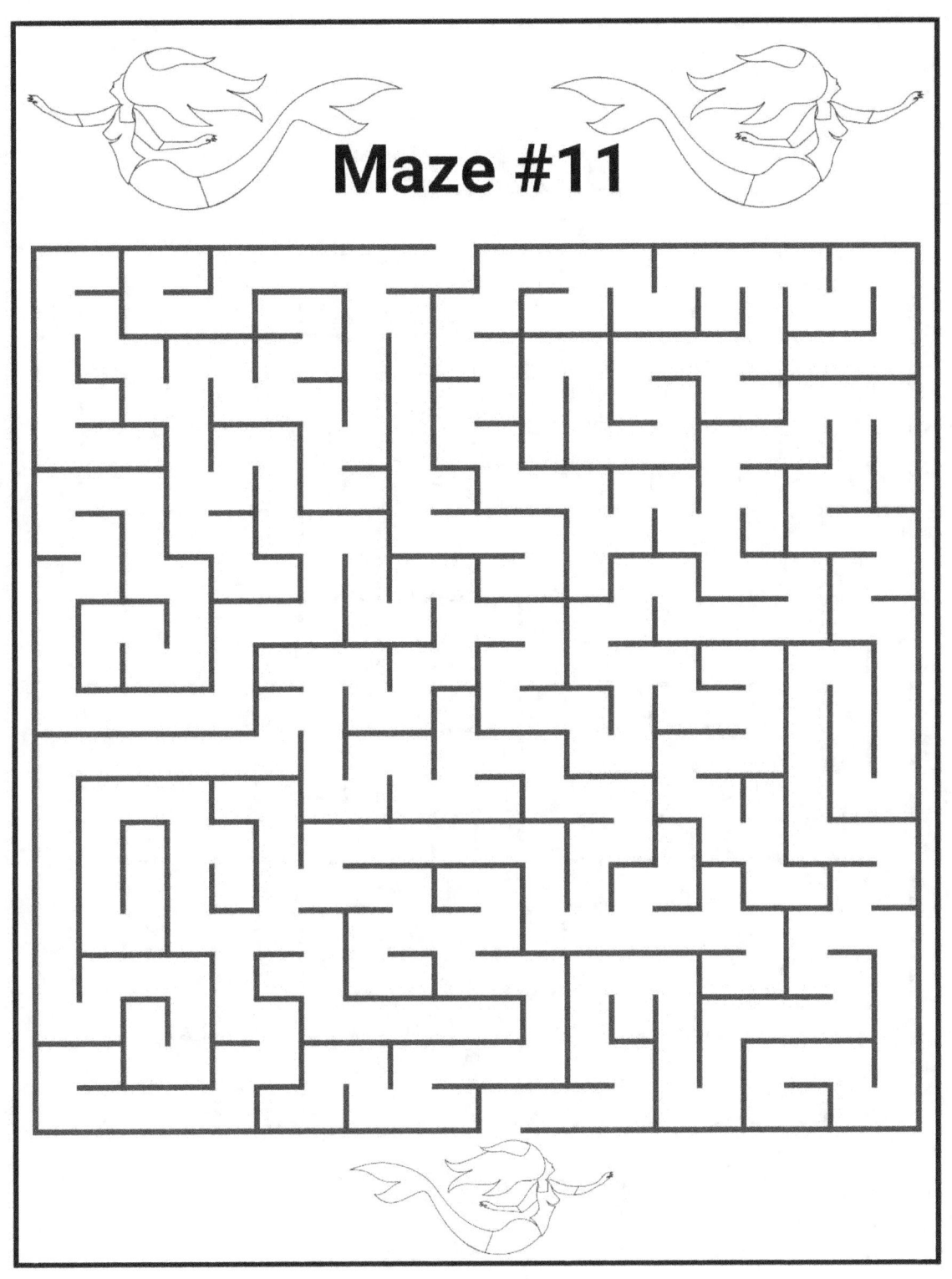

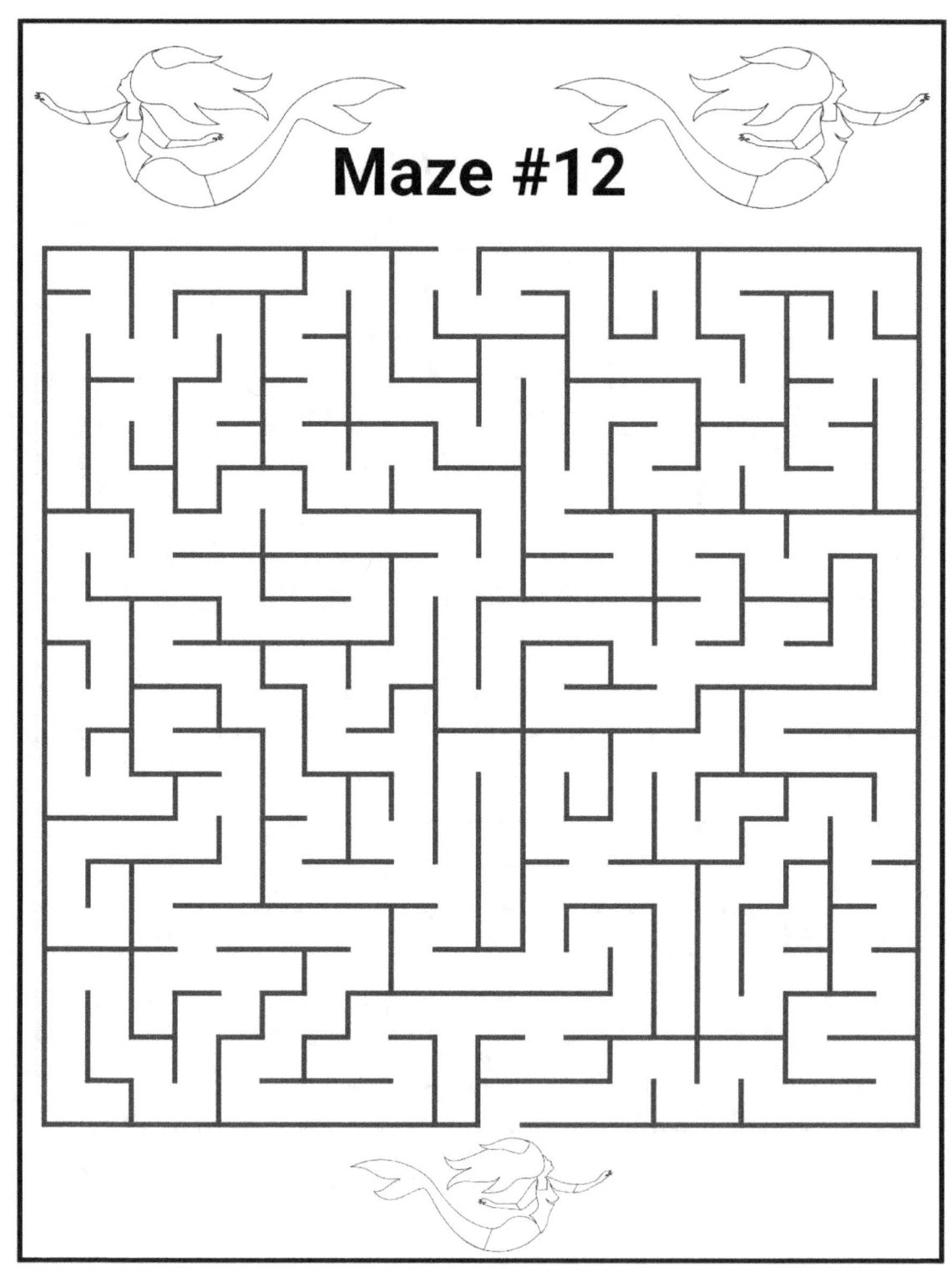

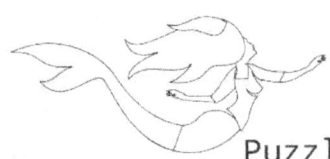

Puzzle #1

1	8	2	9	5	7	6	4	3
6	3	7	2	4	8	5	1	9
5	9	4	6	3	1	2	7	8
2	1	8	3	7	4	9	5	6
9	7	5	1	2	6	3	8	4
3	4	6	5	8	9	7	2	1
4	5	9	8	6	2	1	3	7
8	2	1	7	9	3	4	6	5
7	6	3	4	1	5	8	9	2

Puzzle #2

1	8	5	6	7	4	3	9	2
3	2	9	5	1	8	6	7	4
6	7	4	2	9	3	1	8	5
8	5	6	1	3	9	4	2	7
2	1	7	4	8	6	5	3	9
4	9	3	7	2	5	8	6	1
9	4	2	8	6	1	7	5	3
5	3	8	9	4	7	2	1	6
7	6	1	3	5	2	9	4	8

Puzzle #3

9	7	4	1	3	5	6	2	8
2	3	1	4	8	6	9	5	7
8	5	6	9	7	2	4	1	3
6	8	2	7	4	1	5	3	9
1	9	3	6	5	8	7	4	2
7	4	5	3	2	9	8	6	1
3	2	9	8	6	4	1	7	5
5	6	8	2	1	7	3	9	4
4	1	7	5	9	3	2	8	6

Puzzle #4

4	2	3	1	5	6	7	9	8
9	6	7	4	2	8	3	1	5
5	1	8	3	7	9	6	2	4
7	3	6	8	9	5	2	4	1
8	4	1	2	3	7	9	5	6
2	5	9	6	4	1	8	3	7
6	9	2	7	1	4	5	8	3
1	8	5	9	6	3	4	7	2
3	7	4	5	8	2	1	6	9

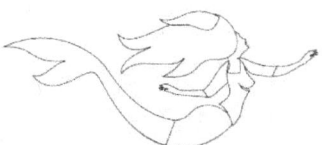

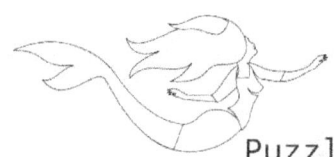

Puzzle #5

9	6	7	4	5	3	8	2	1
5	8	3	6	1	2	9	4	7
2	1	4	7	9	8	6	3	5
3	2	5	8	6	7	4	1	9
6	4	9	1	2	5	3	7	8
8	7	1	9	3	4	2	5	6
7	5	2	3	8	6	1	9	4
4	9	6	2	7	1	5	8	3
1	3	8	5	4	9	7	6	2

Puzzle #6

5	7	8	2	6	1	4	3	9
3	4	9	7	8	5	1	6	2
1	2	6	9	4	3	5	7	8
7	5	3	4	2	6	8	9	1
4	8	2	1	9	7	6	5	3
6	9	1	5	3	8	2	4	7
9	6	4	3	1	2	7	8	5
2	3	7	8	5	4	9	1	6
8	1	5	6	7	9	3	2	4

Puzzle #7

8	4	6	5	2	1	3	7	9
3	1	5	4	9	7	8	6	2
2	7	9	8	3	6	4	1	5
9	6	3	2	7	8	5	4	1
5	2	4	1	6	3	9	8	7
1	8	7	9	5	4	6	2	3
6	9	2	7	4	5	1	3	8
4	5	8	3	1	2	7	9	6
7	3	1	6	8	9	2	5	4

Puzzle #8

7	4	2	6	5	8	1	3	9
8	6	3	1	2	9	4	7	5
1	5	9	7	3	4	8	6	2
3	7	5	4	8	1	9	2	6
2	9	1	3	6	5	7	4	8
6	8	4	2	9	7	3	5	1
5	1	7	9	4	6	2	8	3
4	3	8	5	1	2	6	9	7
9	2	6	8	7	3	5	1	4

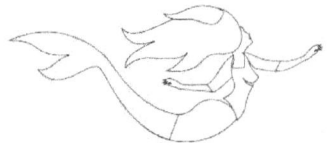

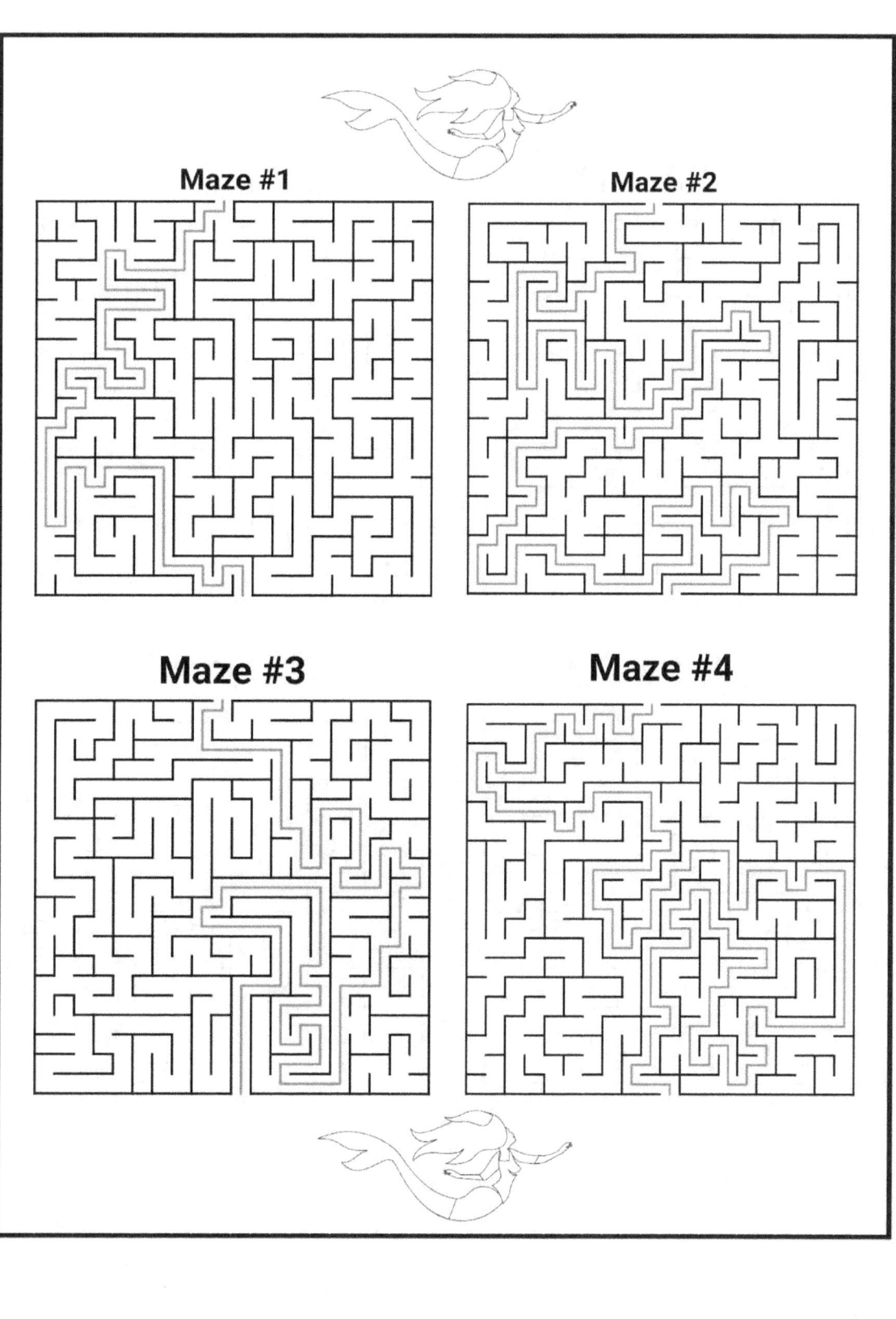

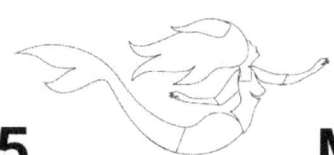

Maze #5

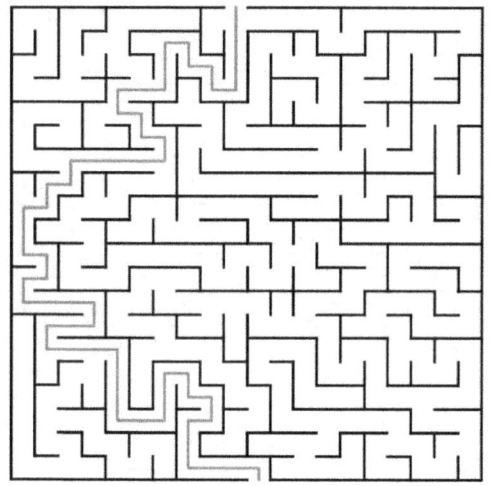

Maze #6

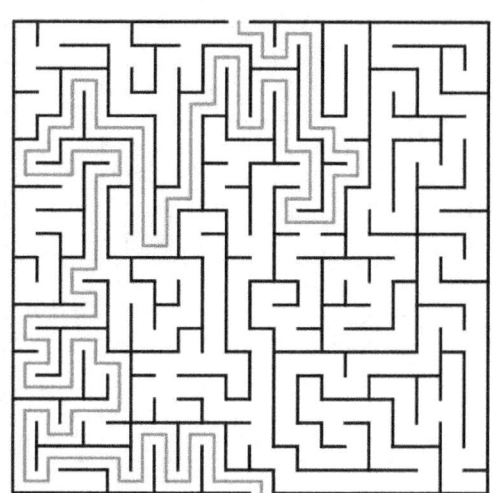

Maze #7

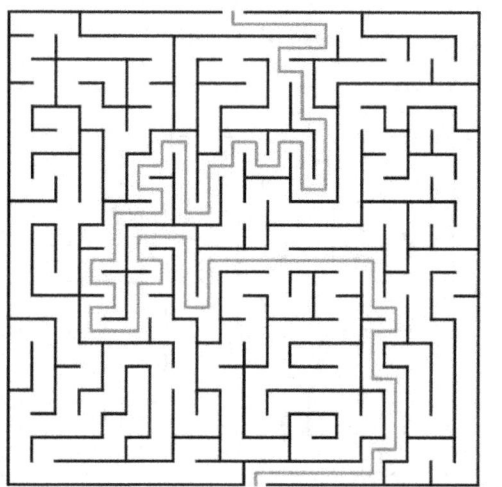

Maze #8

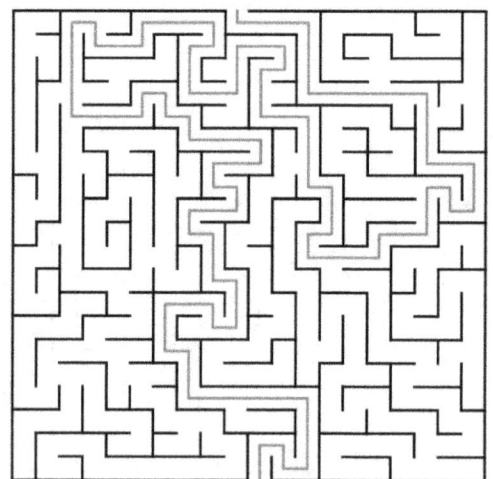

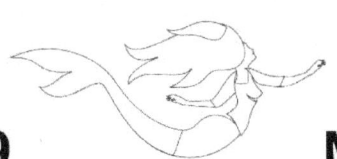

Maze #9

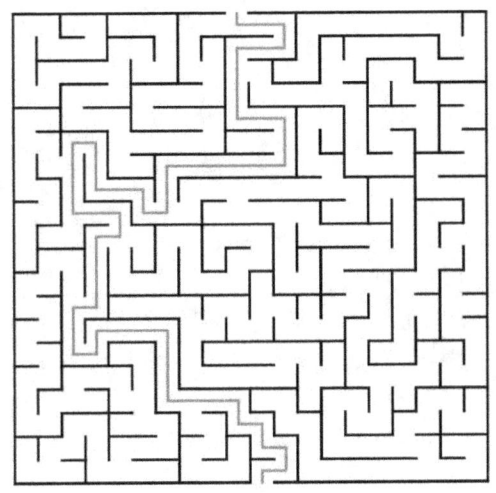

Maze #10

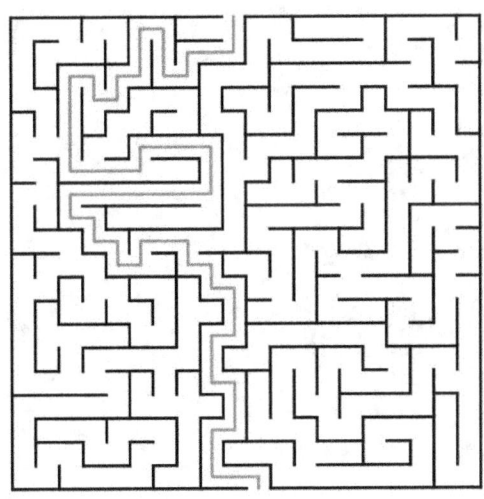

Maze #11

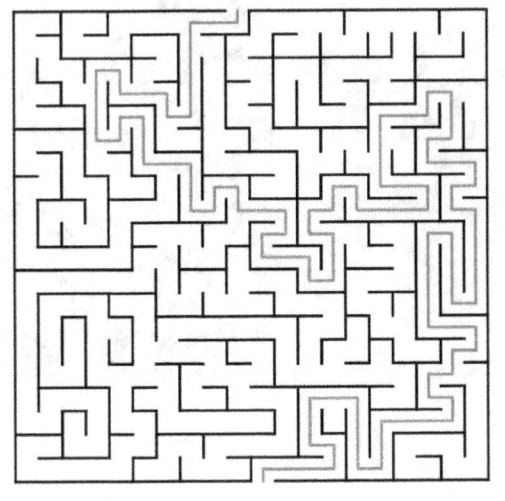

Maze #12

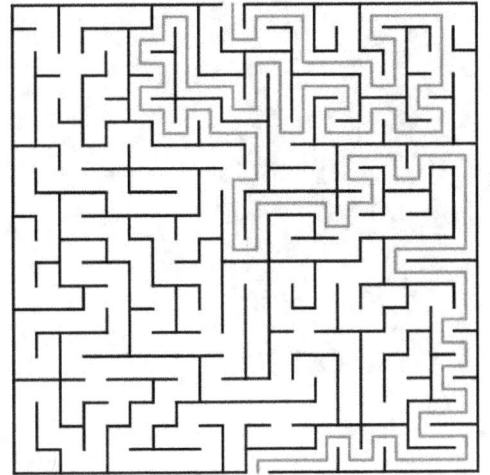

CHILDREN'S BOOKS BY MELISSA CAUDLE

Melissa Caudle has more adult coloring books available on Amazon, Barnes and Noble, and online retailers. You may also go to her website at: www.drmelissacaudle.com

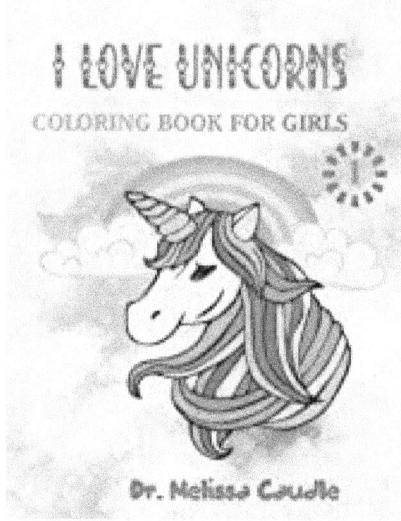
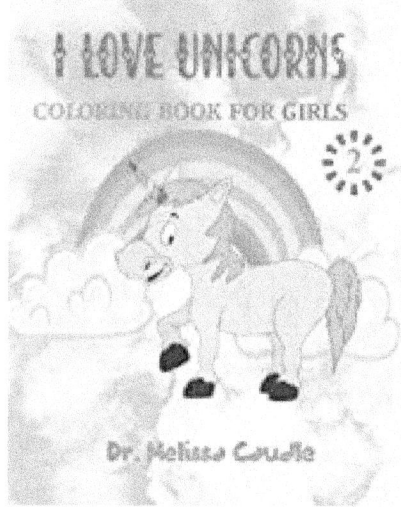
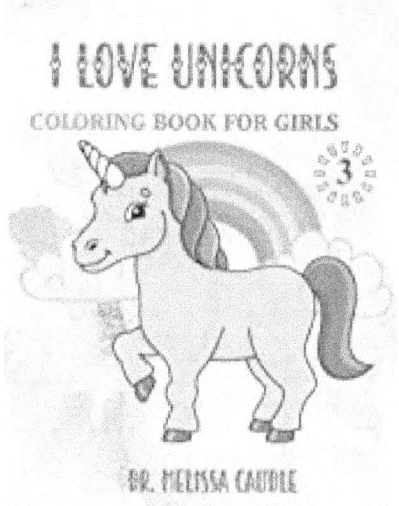
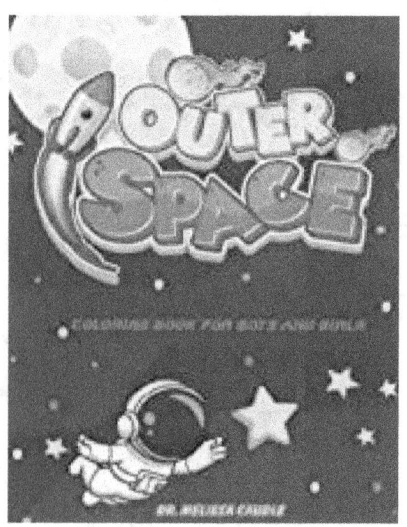
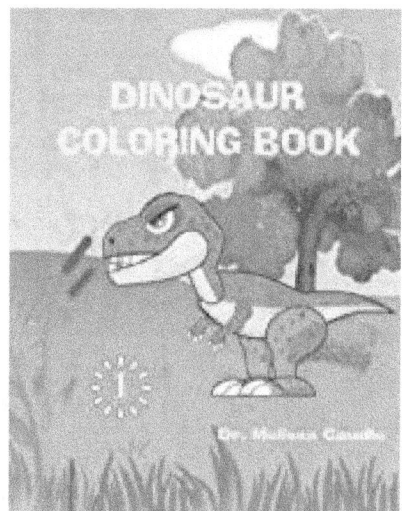
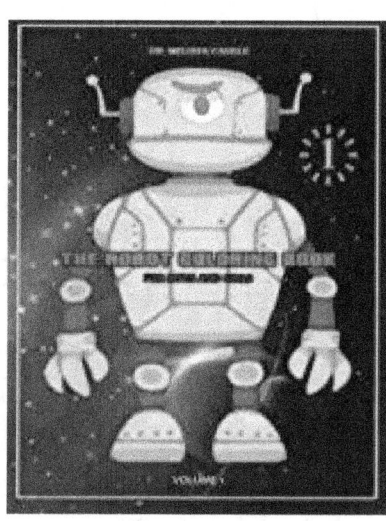
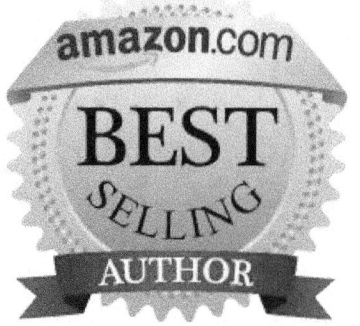

THE AMAZINGLY
Fun Jumbo Activity
BOOK FOR KIDS

Crossword Puzzles, Mazes, Color by Numbers, Wordsearch, Spot the Difference, Tracing, Unscramble the Words, Connect the Dots, Identify Shapes, Matching, and More Fun Stuff

AN AWARD-WINNING PRINCIPAL OF THE YEAR
DR. MELISSA CAUDLE

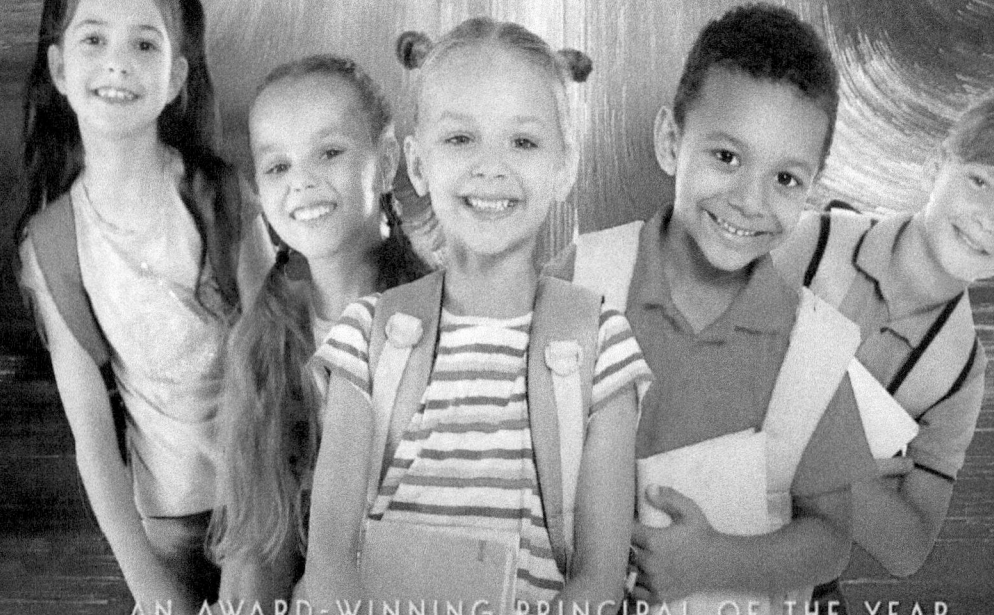

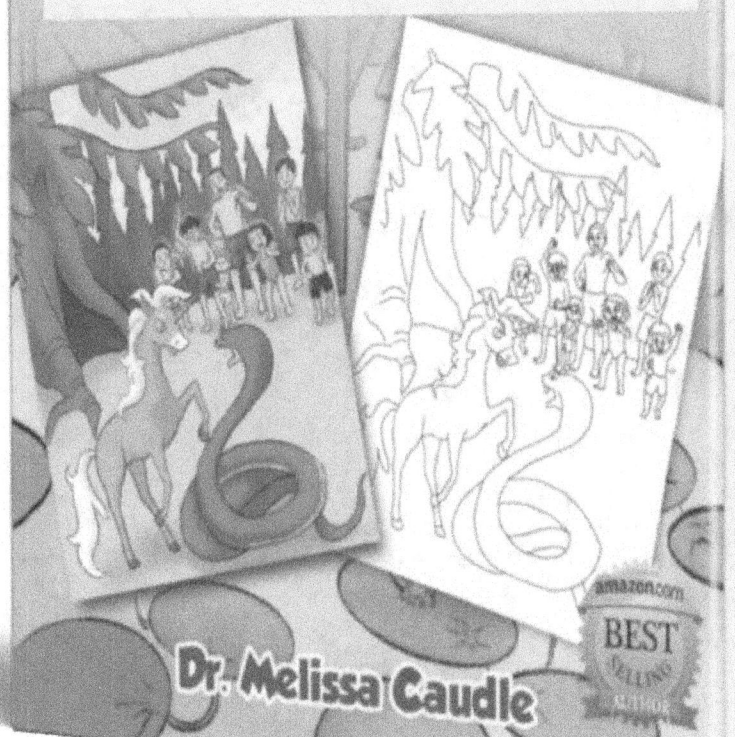

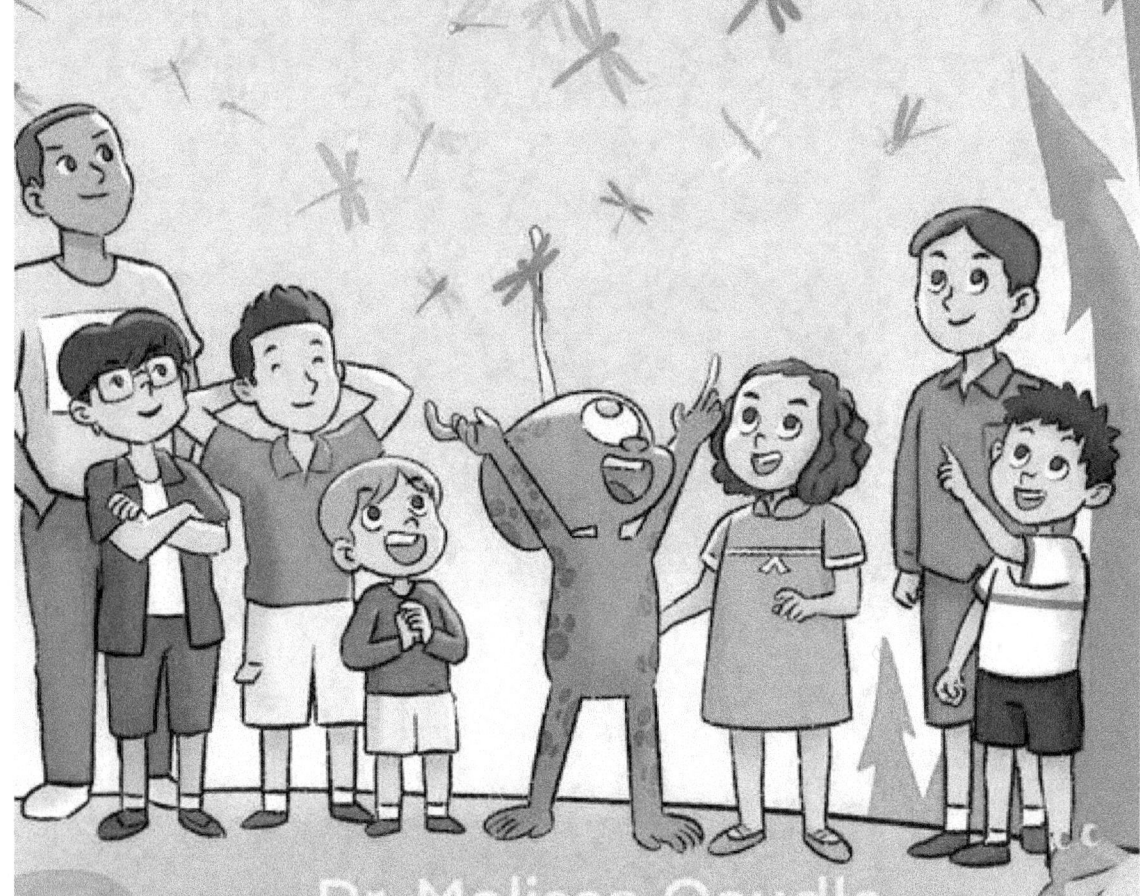

#1 Best Seller

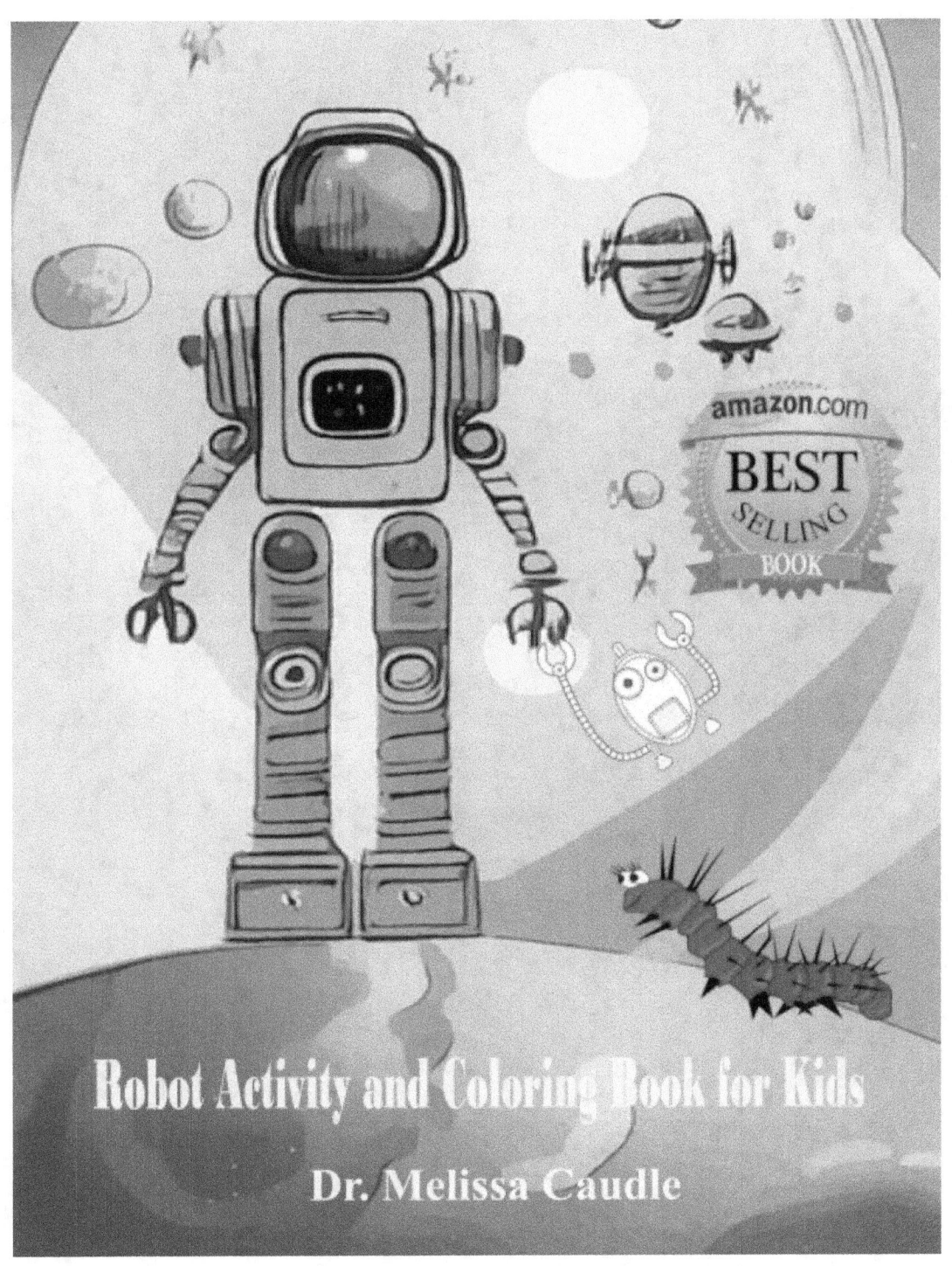

#1 Best Seller

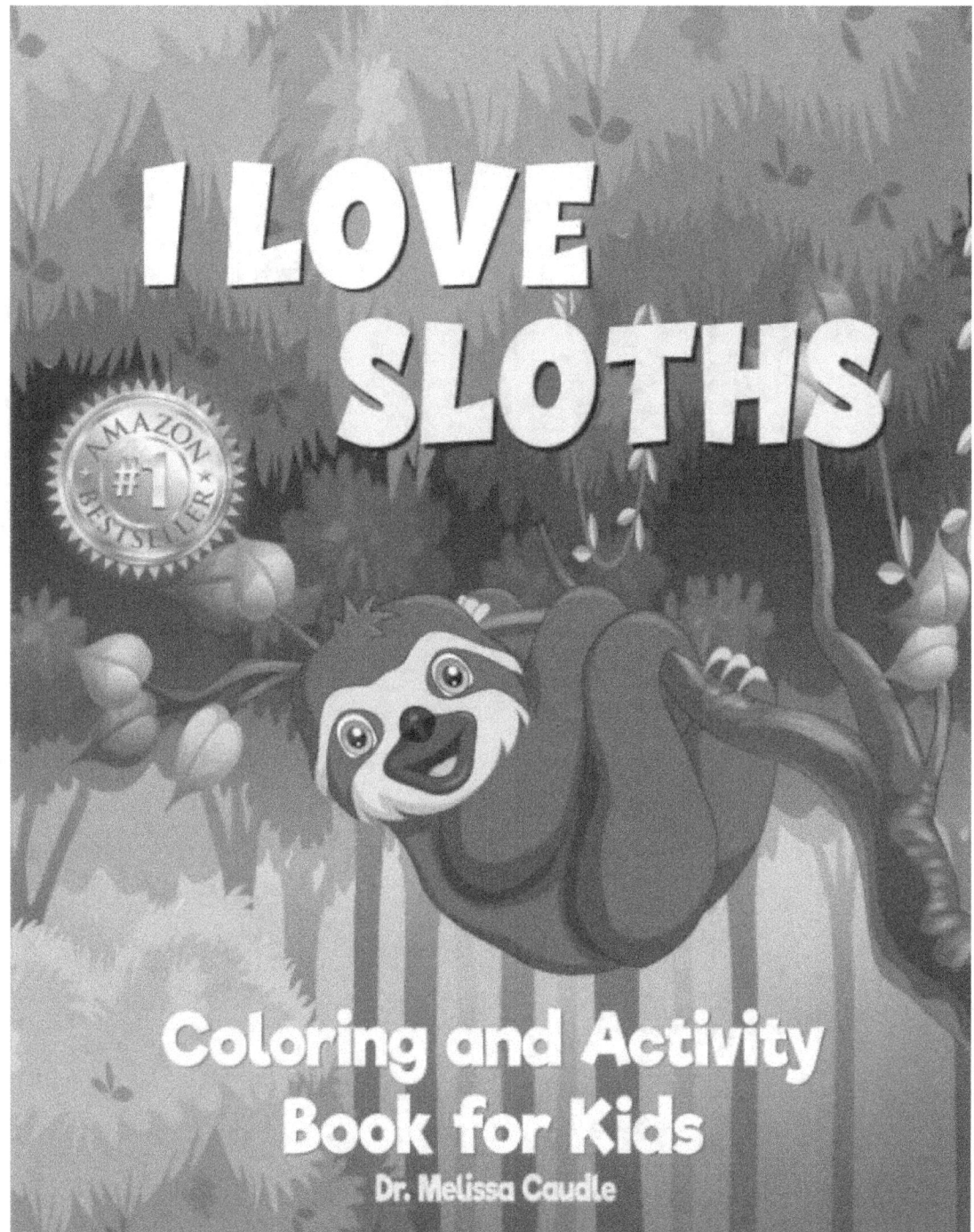

#1 Best Seller

Happy Holidays

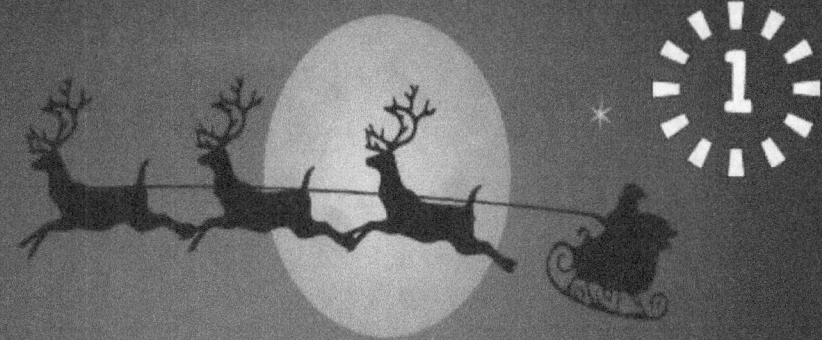

ACTIVITY & COLORING BOOK FOR KIDS

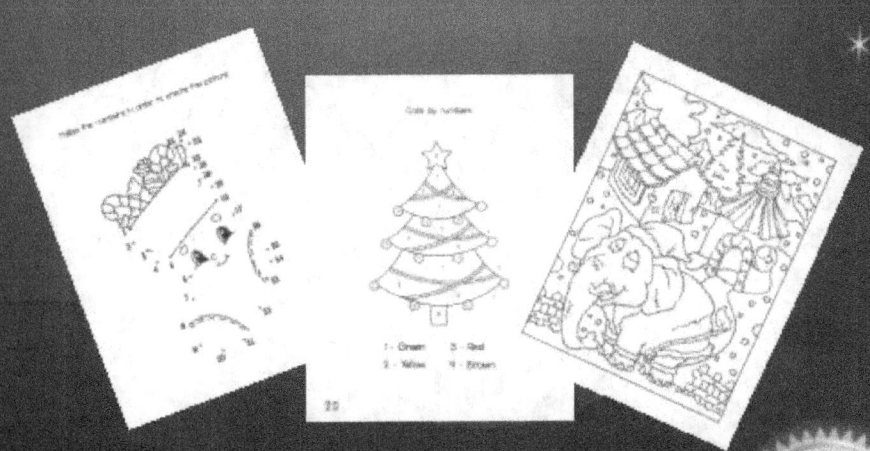

Dr. Melissa Caudle

#1 Best Seller

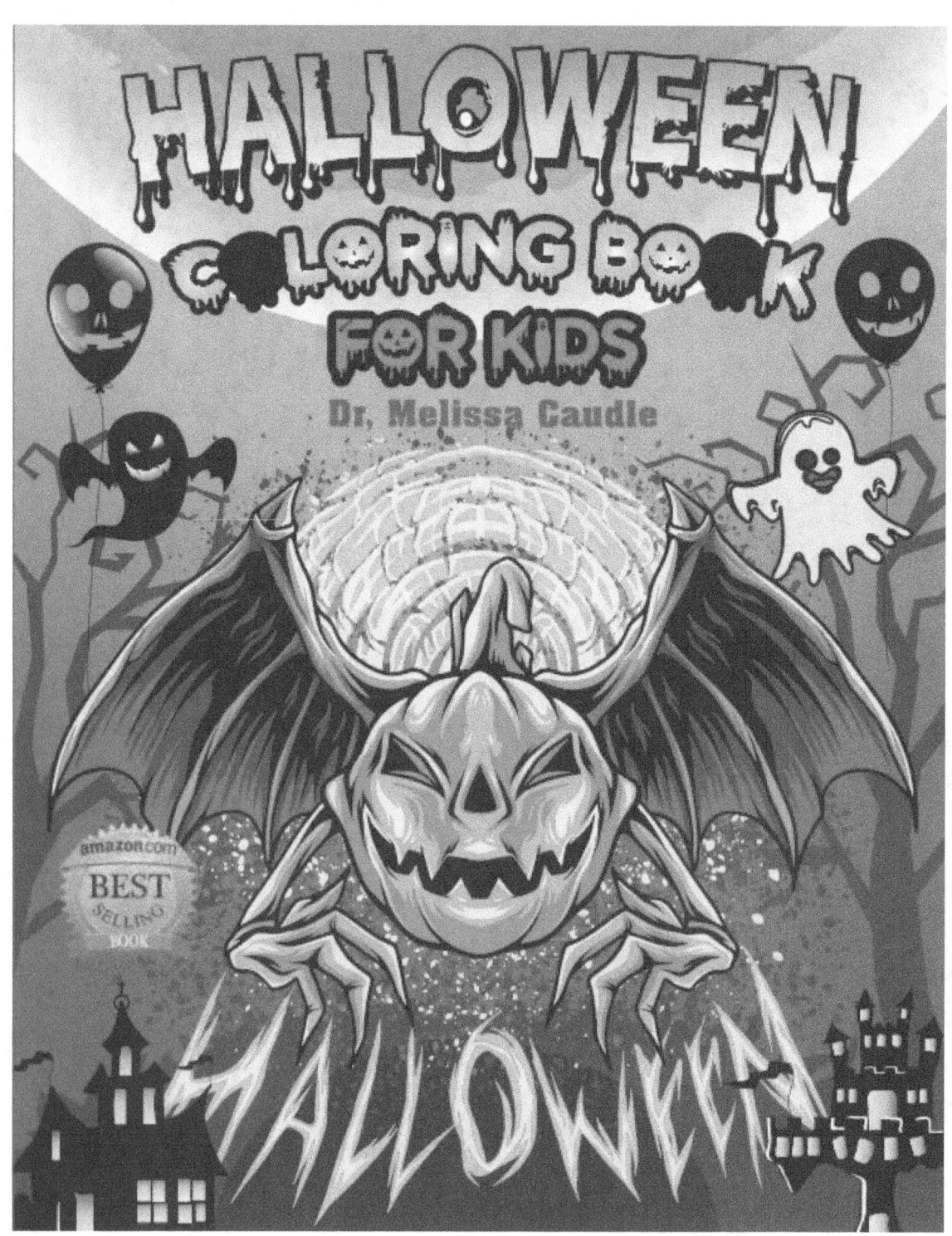

#1 Best Seller